the
book
of
survival

the
book
of
survival

Everyman's guide to staying alive
and handling emergencies in the city, the suburbs
and the wild lands beyond

by Anthony Greenbank

Harper & Row, Publishers
New York and Evanston

This book was originally published in England.

FIRST U.S. EDITION 1968

LIBRARY OF CONGRESS CATALOG CARD NUMBER: 67-28832

All the following advice presupposes that
whoever faces catastrophe takes a deep breath
and makes up his mind to have a really
determined go at beating the odds

CONTENTS

ILLUSTRATIONS

PREFACE

This book is about how to survive. How to live through almost every conceivable accident or disaster that our dangerous world can produce.

Accidents and disasters, of course, *can't* happen to you. But they do. Every day. To thousands of people like you, whose only really nightmarish experience was their last.

Fires, floods, earthquakes, out-of-control cars, crashing trains, sinking ships ask no questions. Wind, rain, snow, ice, burning sun make no exemptions. Lost in a mountain mist, wandering thirst-crazed in a desert, freezing to death in a blizzard, the fact that it can't happen to you makes no difference. It *is* happening.

When it does happen, you probably won't have this book in your coat pocket. You'll be lucky if you have a coat at all. But after reading this book you will be mentally equipped. Equipped to escape the immediate danger. Equipped to stay breathing until help arrives. Equipped to survive.

To live through an impossible situation, you don't need the reflexes of a Grand Prix driver, the muscles of a Hercules, the mind of an Einstein. You simply need to know what to do.

This book is the first of its kind. The first textbook of what, in an increasingly complex and dangerous world, has become a new science.

The book contains nothing but information. Tight-packed, factual information. No cheap thrills. No heroes. No heroics. Just hard facts. Which, we hope, will enable many youngsters to live to be parents, many parents to live to be grandparents and many grandparents to live out, peacefully, their natural life span.

INTRODUCTION

The Book of Survival is like no other. It gives a man, his wife and his children a fighting chance in any catastrophe at a time when—as any newspaper will tell you—the chances are they will succumb and die. It is not a do-it-yourself James Bond manual, for it assumes no advance preparation except reading it.

People ARE growing softer today. Elements of modern-day living not only make us more vulnerable: They fatten for the kill. Read the headlines: *Careering car wipes out newlyweds; runaway train annihilates 37 commuters; crowd at spectator sport crushes 9; flaming electric blanket murders family; unseen knifing in dark discotheque; veering plane massacres 24 vacationers* . . .

Existing survival books go strongly on the mountain, desert, jungle, arctic and ocean scene. They are useless to the family facing an onrushing tide and trapped by cliffs, or to the salesman whose car is trapped among snowdrifts miles from anywhere. Not only are they unlikely to have read them: If they had, the pertinent information—wrapped among graphs, tables, case histories, maps and bibliographies—would be almost impossible to recollect.

Most of us have only the vaguest idea of survival. If thought about at all, it is by some quaint rule of thumb (does one pour gasoline on frostbitten fingers—NO!). We face the bitterest winters at home with equanimity—and are surprised, shocked and hurt when threats of exposure and frostbite turn into a reality.

This book deals with *crises*. Prevention is better than cure, but no one is immune from human or mechanical failure, or Act of God. Hence the stress on *when* catastrophe hits home—*when* car is submarining to bottom of lake, *when* intruders are binding you hand and foot, *when* eyes are blinded. Where possible, prevention is treated too—in note form.

People would never remember in a crisis? Not usually so! Fed with a drill to save its skin, the brain grabs that plan by the scruff of the neck. True, the girl whose arms are already pinned by an assailant cannot produce the comb which might save her, but let her hear him first padding behind along the pavement and she could.

Instead of being mesmerized with fright, you are more likely to be ready and braced in a sudden crisis after reading this book than before. In a fight for life lasting weeks your subconscious would automatically reach back for help from its pages. To this end, mnemonics (memory-fixers) are incorporated in the very layout of the book by using entry headings unique in survival tracts to date.

Human feelings are the key. Pitched into catastrophe they cry for warmth or cold or water or dry land or shade or light or speed or slowness regardless of whether dazzling glare is from H-bomb or head-lights, stifling heat is in desert or burning house, choking contamination is radiation or carbon monoxide. This book is arranged to rally these feelings by grouping remedies under them: fire making under *TOO COLD,* car-collision drill under *TOO FAST.* And so on.

No entry here presumes that you are prepared. When crisis looms—*that's it!* There are YOU (bone/skin/hair/teeth/nails/saliva), your possessions (shoes/socks/pants/skirt/dress/watch/possibly cash, comb, etc.), the surroundings (sand/rock/water/trees/concrete/guano) and quite often wrecked transportation (car/plane/train/boat). Desert captives are not allowed to find a handy sheet of plastic for a water still, though if they have one already, its use is shown—but well down the list of water-seeking methods.

The theme of this book is not so much "be prepared" as *be prepared to improvise with anything.* When "everything" seems so slight as to be ridiculous, think of rescuers saying: "If only he'd wrapped up in those newspapers. . . ." This book takes it for granted you have nothing rather than something . . . but if you have something, use it.

Using this book we suggest you (a) anticipate trouble ahead in likely places (football game/plane flight/rush-hour traffic) by check-ing in the index under such headings, then turning to the relevant pages for advance briefing; (b) read the book more than once so that in sudden fire/flood/tempest/earthquake you increase your chances of surviving. And as an extra aid the entries are linked by cross-refer-ences: Climbing from sea into boat comes in *TOO LOW,* but getting to that boat happens in *TOO WET.* Hence there is a cross-reference to link them.

Survivors will always live to tell of surviving by doing just the opposite of others who have also survived. Medical experts have often told survivors that by all rights they should be dead. Instead of dying they had the WILL to live. YOU TOO MUST ENLIST THIS WILL, that sense of self-preservation which starts with a deep breath and the determination not to give way at any cost.

People are growing softer today—yes; but it is a cheering fact that, given a plan of action, even though despairing and shocked, people can and do react well in crises. Once the initial shock has lessened you stand every chance of becoming a *survivor* if, as we suggest, you give yourself a regular servicing by rereading this, a kind of maintenance handbook.

1: TOO LONELY

Anyone facing extinction feels the loneliest person on earth. You are as alone in the rioting football crowd squashing air from your lungs as on a raft at sea.

The anatomy of loneliness is a skeleton. Jerking muscles, scrabbling fingers, shivering marrow, straining sinews—these are the bare bones of panic and initial despair.

"Survival of the fittest" does not mean you have to be physically perfect. Stripped to a clawing puppet by crisis, everyone is reduced to an isolation where survival is all in the mind.

ASPECTS OF LONELINESS

MENTAL

TAKING A DEEP BREATH AND MAKING UP YOUR MIND TO HAVE A REALLY DETERMINED GO AT BEATING THE ODDS AT ALL COSTS IS THE VITAL FACTOR IN SURVIVAL.

When initial shock brings utter despair, it is still possible for that sense of self-preservation to pull you through, though you may be totally disoriented and terrified.

If contemplating giving in or suicide, prayer is a proven help. *The Lord is My Shepherd . . . Though I Walk Through the Valley of the Shadow of Death . . . Thy Rod and Thy Staff They Comfort Me . . .* the Twenty-third Psalm is a proven favorite (most can remember words in some form or other). So is the Lord's Prayer.

Other pleas range from the Catholic's *O my God, relying on Thy infinite goodness . . .* and the Jewish *Hear, O Israel, the Lord our God . . .* to a universal *O God, get us out of this mess.*

Run/drive/signal/swim/make fires/build shelter/ signal again . . . *all the harder*. Don't lie down to die without a fantastic struggle first. Never ever give in.

Tell yourself: *Even this will pass.*

1

In unknown environment: Improvise, improvise, improvise.

Never never never never never never never never never give up trying. Out of all the untidiness, quickness and/or dragging slowness of survival, salvage, clutch and spur your vital instinct of self-preservation.

DESPERATION

Alcoholics Anonymous. National Save-a-Life League. Rescue. Crisis Clinic . . . all are organizations, available by telephone (look under SUICIDE in phone directory), which have prevented suicides when contacted by someone in deep trouble.

Telephone operators will help in such circumstances all over the world, supplying you with the needed local information.

CLAUSTROPHOBIA

VERY unpleasant feeling. The real thing grips trapped people with panic. Will do something rash/scream/kick/hammer place down/rave/fight. Very few suffer from real claustrophobia; very many think they do.

Restrain anyone so gripped with fear (so they don't hurt themselves or you). Comfort. Calm. Reassure. Only slap in face or render unconscious if situation out of control.

Count blessings. One—I'm alive. Two—(probably) not injured. Three—can last several days without food and water so long as not using energy. Four—only a matter of time before they find me. Five —keep keeping cool.

Check pockets/handbag/surroundings for food/matches/keys/nail file/lighter—anything that may help to scratch/dig/screw/signal way out.

Improvise lavatory from stones/holes/rubbish/clothing to cover. If nothing (say in elevator), make sponge from clothing/newspaper, etc.

AGORAPHOBIA

Fear of open or public places (rarer than claustrophobia) also brings terror. Dizziness/sickness/fainting seizes victims. Can come gradually or in sudden panic.

It is no cure to be told to "Snap out of it."

Get INSIDE (bus/shop/cinema) if attacked by agoraphobia. Buy magazine and bury head in it until you get home.

If prone to attacks always carry a dime for a telephone call for help to friends or relatives.

IMAGINATION

Terror can mount in the dark/gloom/shade (see *TOO DARK*).

Fight it down. Get a grip. Rationalize the things-that-go-bump/things-that-go-flash/things-that-touch-you. They usually have ordinary explanations.

As with, for example, a lonely house you are beginning to feel is haunted. The following are likely causes:

House is built above underground watercourse.

Machinery in locality sets up vibrations.

Echoes from next door.

Roof/walls/floors expanding or contracting.

Tight-fitting doors making air traps of each room.

Reflections from passing cars/trains/planes.

Tree branches scraping on window.

Cats/mice/starlings-in-the-attic.

Green wood in house structure groans and creaks.

Slate off roof makes wind moan.

Air lock in water pipes makes thumping noise.

To reassure yourself make a ghost-check when daylight comes. Inspect all house (cupboards/chimneys/attic). Seal off rooms and windows. Tie black cotton across stairs/landings/doors. Pans of water on floors show vibrations. Shake dust/sand/powder on floors.

Final consolation: A REAL ghost

(a) Will disappear if you approach it.

(b) Can do you no physical harm because it leaves nothing earthly —not even messages or footprints.

(c) Will not cast a shadow; will look quite substantial rather than misty; will not ignore you; will not carry its head tucked under an arm.

(d) Is all in YOUR mind anyway.

HOW TO GET HELP

How *do* you call HELP! successfully today when the tendency is for passers-by to cross to the other side of the road in case you are (a) part of the TV Candid Camera team, (b) going to make them look foolish anyway; (c) going to get them killed? How *do* you say SOS successfully miles from civilization?

USE EVERYTHING. Screams. Whispers. Shouts. Sign language. Whistles. Bonfires. Matchlight. Bang central-heating pipes/car horn/ doors. Wave clothes. Flash mirror. Throw stones. Keep whistling kettle on boil. Toll bell. Blow bugle. Smash glass. Fly kite. Pull emergency cord. Light candle. Bang head/shoes/fists on wall.

(Note: Don't endanger *yourself*. For example, rush to toll church bell unschooled in the art and you will be rocketed up by rope to crack skull on ceiling.)

PECULIAR CRISES—UNORTHODOX SIGNALS. Trapped on moonlit roof yank away TV aerials. Giving Kiss of Life in express-train compartment throw note (weighted with ballpoint pen) on passing station platform begging ambulance ready at next stop (pulling emergency cord would waste time). On tailboard of speeding hi-jacked truck, go mad until some driver slows, winds window down and you shout POLICE!

DON'T RELY ON ONE METHOD. Yell *and* shake curtain. Whistle *and* flick cigarette lighter. Whisper to garage attendant that your passenger has gun *and* break law in front of police car. Use sign language *and* break glass. Light fire *and* wave. Erect red triangle on road *and* set fire to oily rags.

PICK BEST POSITION (if possible). By window. On higher ground. On open snow field. By chink blowing draft through roof-collapse rubble. Under gap in treetop canopy. On boat's mast.

SELECT YOUR SIGNALS. Save energy (shouting and waving), flashlight batteries, matches, bonfire fuel when far from view and earshot until help approaches. Keep them in reserve, dry and ready to use instantly. Meanwhile signal with: flags, markers, shadow writing, dust clouds, mirror.

NEVER GIVE UP. Keep signaling until answered no matter how long that is.

WAYS OF SIGNALING

FLAGS

Rip sheets, shirts, coat linings—any material not used directly for clothing or shelter. Fly flags from sticks, poles, windows, roofs, conspicuous trees. More chance of success when waved. Try for contrast with background: red, orange, yellow against snow, or dirt-smeared cloth if only white available. Keep it flying all the time. Fly a kite when you have line/handkerchief/wind. Practice—a distress kite can carry a fishing line too (see *TOO EMPTY*). Note: Twigs/saplings/wire/framework are "bowed" away from cloth.

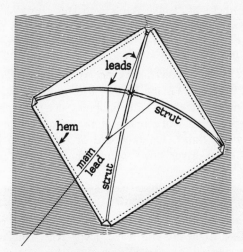

Kite made from handkerchief and twigs

MARKERS

Use anything that is static to draw attention. Crashed plane, beached boat, stranded car. They are better seen from the air if the top surfaces are clean and—where applicable—polished. Clear away snow, sand, foliage. Trample, ravage, spoil and burn surroundings to make conspicuous. Spread rocks into noticeable formations. Deposit rubbish to litter the scene. Lay anything that glints or is bright on top of plane or vehicle. Polish bright surfaces with sand or gravel.

Important:

(a) *Getting out* from a crash scene far from civilization is always to be desired and preferred to digging in/making wooden spoons/playing boy scout.

But ONLY leave the marker of plane (or other transport) wreck in favor of trekking for help if you stand a good chance of reaching inhabited farm/igloos/tents/huts/hydro-electric power station/shooting lodge/settlement/town/city.

AND *ONLY* IF YOU ARE IN FIT ENOUGH STATE TO TRAVEL, IF NO CHANCE AT ALL OF BEING SEEN ON CRASH SITE FROM THE AIR AND IF YOU MAKE PREPARATIONS FIRST FOR THE TREK OUT (see *TOO SLOW*).

Otherwise stay until found. Very many have died after forsaking immobilized transportation for a desperate cross-country trip.

(b) If living in snow holes or soundproof shelters which blanket the sound of passing aircraft, always, if conditions permit, have someone "on watch" in an open-topped shelter right among the markers to listen and possibly to mirror-flash too.

WRITING

With nail polish/keys/pebble/nail file/soot/blood/charcoal/cinders/soap/grease . . . on slate/stone/dirty car/inner birch bark/walls/cloth/plastic/tin . . . in dust/snow/sand/mud.

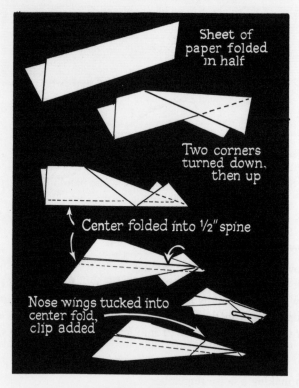

Sheet of paper folded in half

Two corners turned down, then up

Center folded into ½" spine

Nose wings tucked into center fold, clip added

SOS airplane

Write SOS on glass (if not in position to smash it) with finger/
fingernail/lipstick if glass is clear/misted/frosted. To make it readable
from other side write ZOZ (and round off Z's to make turnabout S's).
Also write ! ꟼ⅃ƎH And add anything to qualify: ƎᴚƎH ᴎI ƎVI⅃A
MA

Write SOS message on paper and fold it into a dart (as shown).
Flight it for busiest street, say, when trapped high in a building.

On a bigger scale, and miles from anywhere:

Shuffle out letters SOS (shadow writing) 20 to 30 feet tall in
snow. Deepen tracks into broad channels, and pile the snow from these
where they will cast the sun into long shadows along the letters. Increase size of these drifts with underlayer of rocks. Stress shadows
with soil, leaves, branches, stones. A good shadow sign can be seen
from airplane on moonlit night.

Shadow writing

Shadow writing can be used in sand.

Where neither snow nor sand, use rocks, tree branches and sods to
build low walls to shadow letters SOS. Again sculpt for shadows with
leaves, debris, soil in the shadow areas. Shovel any patches of snow
(as may exist in timber country) into letters to stress shadows.

NOISE

When making a noise remember
(a) Shout only when likely to be heard (say when stuck in old-

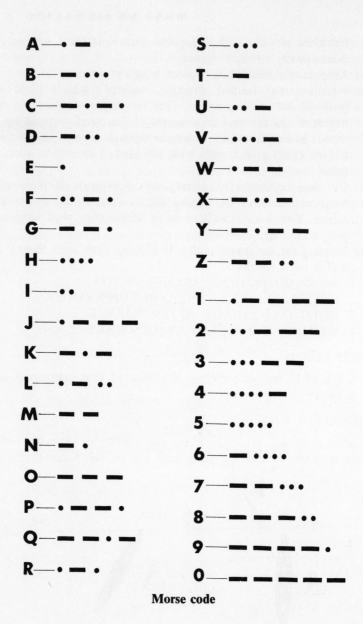

Morse code

fashioned elevator with collapsible gates). It takes up energy/makes thirsty/roughens throat.

(b) Keep quiet at intervals to hear any sound of others.

(c) Whistle carries furthest. Practice shepherd's whistle while imprisoned and awaiting rescue. (Put two fingers—either first two fingers or the first and third fingers of one hand—against tip of tongue in mouth and try to whistle through narrow gap of these fingers. Don't press tongue back too hard. You may be successful in time.)

(d) Use best conductor of sound—say, tapping metal pipes with hand-held dentures (if nothing else)—when buried in building rubble. You don't HAVE to know Morse code. Just keep tapping/scratching/thumping.

(e) Smash glass for sound outlet. If nothing (not even shoes) for a club use a fist thus:

1. WRAP SOMETHING AROUND WRIST.
2. PUNCH STRAIGHT—KNUCKLES UPPERMOST.
3. HOLD FIST STEADY AFTER IMPACT.
4. WITHDRAW HAND VERY GINGERLY.

DUST CLOUD

Stir sand or dust into column if chance of help approaches *and* it is calm.

SIGNALING MIRROR

Most vital aid. An opened tin can substitutes. Punch ⅛-inch hole in center of can top (this need not be taken completely off

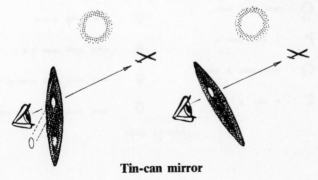

Tin-can mirror

the can if you don't want to remove it). Hold up to face and sight airplane below sun. The sun spot which falls on your cheek via the hole can then be bounced back through hole at aircraft so long as (1) you hold plane in sight; (2) *tilt tin lid so that sun spot disappears into hole.* Note: Reflection must be on both sides of mirror for your face must be reflected on one side of the tin (so you can see the sun spot), and the sun must be reflected from the other side.

Keep flashing even at empty view: Flash can be seen miles away by aircraft. Ease off if plane nears into intermittent flashes so as not to dazzle.

BONFIRE

(See also *TOO COLD*). Day and night use. If fuel scarce then hoard the material under stones, branches, leaves, soil, grass until a plane or ship passes. Then light quickly. Rock or log platform underneath fire helps. Keep gasoline (if available) standing by to boost flames. Build more than one signal fire if possible. Keep checking them during bad weather. Kindling can be kept dry by body warmth.

SMOKE SIGNALS

Has to be a calm day. Use (1) white smoke on clear days by adding moss, green foliage, sprinkling fire with urine; (2) black smoke for gloomy days by burning rubber (floor mats/tires), oil or oily rags. But ensure you have a good fire first, not easily snuffed out.

PARACHUTE TEPEE

A kind of wigwam made from branches and parachute fabric (see *TOO COLD*). You can burn a fire *inside* to convert shelter into beacon.

FLASHLIGHT

Save flashlight battery until chance of rescue nears. Even small flashlight shows up well in open country at night. Keep it moving. Reflect circle of light on snow or bright reflector as well as pointing flashlight at sky or horizon.

Wave flaming spruce branch, or bunches of lit-up dried and knotted grass, or burning oil rags on stick.

Whole spruce tree makes excellent torch when ignited if (a) conspicuously placed, (b) thick-branched, (c) you make a bird's nest of intertwined dead branches low down in the center, (d) you shield this with leaves, spare fabric, branches, etc. until drone of plane is heard. If tree is snow-covered when you want to light up, keep nest cover in place until you have shaken off snow. Gasoline helps to light. Tips of spruce should flare . . . and show for miles.

MORE POSSIBILITIES

RADIO TRANSMITTER—Use immediately if intact, and while batteries are in working order, by sending distress signals at regular intervals. EMERGENCY TRANSMITTER (when limited range save until possible help approaches). ROCKETS (keep dry until help near). SEA-MARKER DYE (good for staining snow too). GUNSHOT (save until help near). SMOKE FLARES (save too).

DISTRESS SIGNALS

LETTERS "SOS" can be used anywhere: sounded, flashed, smoke-puffed, written. In Morse code the letters become three dots, three dashes, three dots. Pause then repeat.

Some other recognized distress signals are:

1. International Mountain Distress Signal. Six flashes, whistles or waves in a minute, then a minute's silence, then repeat. Rescuing answer is three flashes, whistles or waves a minute, then a minute's silence, then repeat.
2. International Ground–Air Signals. (As shown.) These should qualify the big SOS letters made in shadow writing on snow, sand, soil, grass, shale.
3. International Ground–Air Body Signals. (As shown.)
4. Three fires in a triangle. If fuel is plentiful cover two fires until needed, and use third as camp fire.
5. On boats, signals include: gunshot; flames (from tar or oil barrel, say); a square flag with anything looking like a ball above or below it.

Ground-air signals

GOING FOR HELP

When in a group and an accident has only injured one or some of party (say up mountain/in cave/on island), go for help when route is known/messengers are fit to travel/route for help is possible.

(Note: But only after all party is safe/injured have been given first aid/made as warm as possible.)

Messengers going for help should:
1. BE TWO IN NUMBER IF POSSIBLE—ALWAYS LEAVING ONE PERSON WITH THE INJURED.
2. TAKE WRITTEN MESSAGE GIVING
   Location of injured
   Injuries
   Time of accident
   Number in group
   Help needed
3. GO QUICKLY BUT SAFELY TO NEAREST HABITA-TION/TELEPHONE.
4. WAIT THERE FOR RESCUERS SO THEY CAN GUIDE BACK.

ANSWERING AN SOS

Let survivors know you've seen them. Always answer a distress call if you can help. If you cannot, raise the alarm and try to get help from those who can. It is essential you get the position of survivors—jotting it down on paper as soon as you see or hear SOS if in remote country. Or scratch it on slate, tree bark, metal.

If you can't help directly, it is better to try for extra help than to try to attempt the impossible—which won't help at all. SURVIVAL means your own self-preservation comes first.

IN A TIGHT SPOT

You are never lonelier than when buried alive.
(See also *TOO DARK*.)
Trapped in or by roof-fall, or in any circumstance where there may be a narrow avenue of escape—either to open air or to a position where you can signal for rescue (through chink blowing air)—crawl, wriggle, squeeze or push through.

BUT if safe where you are and you are virtually sure of rescue: *Stay there.* Don't risk precipitating further rubble collapse. Only if no chance of rescue should tentative efforts be made to inch through.

Crawls and squeeze-throughs *can* be safe—say slots, slits and bedding planes in caves unaffected by a roof collapse and possibly offering an escape route when main corridor is blocked.

Such escape routes include porthole/manhole/skylight/squeezes.

Main principles are:

1. Strip off clothing so that if you are forced to back out it doesn't bunch up and cause jamming. Belts with large buckles are dangerous on same count.

2. Most likely person to succeed in wriggling through goes first, following—where possible—any draft of air, or gleam of light.

3. If roof unstable—wait until he gets through. Then follow, handling everything as if it were high explosive. When surroundings are solid, however, wriggle through with hands touching the feet of person in front.

4. A body stiff with tension is more likely to get stuck than one relaxed. Experiment with body positions. Don't rush to get through. Big people can squeeze through amazingly small spaces so long as they relax.

5. Help a stuck person by "talking" him through. Push and pull if physically possible and if captive relaxes.

6. Don't try to yank someone through hole by pulling on a rope, belt or sheet tied around his waist. Could jam him fast. Instead use a hand line. First man through tows string of belts tied together with reef knots. He anchors this at far end. Anyone stuck can then pull themselves along hand over hand. Even so, this *could* lead to muscles tensing, and a jammed person would have to stop and relax to progress.

7. Probably best plan for helping wriggler in difficulty is a loop at the end of the string of belts. Stuck person works foot into

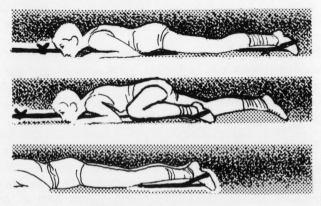

Tight-spot foot-loop rescue

loop and (a) bends at knee of that leg; (b) helpers take in slack of line and anchor it; (c) captive straightens leg squirming forward from its power, then flexes knee again; (d) helpers pull in slack again . . . and so on.

8. Don't try sliding *down* sloping area with arms out ahead—it is almost impossible to get back. Instead try one arm ahead at a time. Or tuck both beneath chest.

9. Where roofs lift a little, stoop with hands on knees. Or go on all fours, and crouch on haunches when resting. Or waddle along on haunches. This keeps knees off the ground.

(IT IS POSSIBLE TO BLACKOUT THROUGH PAIN ON KNEECAPS. THEY ARE NOT DESIGNED TO CARRY THE BODY. BODY HEAT ESCAPES THROUGH THEM ONTO COLD FLOOR, AND CRAWLING ON KNEES OVER ANY DISTANCE IS FAR TOO INEFFICIENT.)

Ways of avoiding wriggling on knees: Lie on outside of leg and hold body up on forearm. Trail other foot behind as you shove forward. Change over to other side for a rest. Or sit on a leg and squirm forward lifting lower thigh and buttock during each thrust.

10. Flat-out crawling and wriggling . . . tuck elbows into sides, hands under shoulders. Or grip fists under chin with elbows nudging solar plexus, and thrust forward with the toes (lift body and knees clear at each reptilian movement). It is not a good plan to reach forward all the time with both hands—for one thing, it usually means your body *drags* along the floor.

LOAD HANDLING

Survival situations call for lifting, pushing, carrying and man-handling (horsing heavy loads around) at all ages and conditions. Try to avoid rupture or slipped disc risk by following these few simple principles.

KEY RULES:

Don't jerk, strain, tug wildly. Think, then p-u-s-h or l-i-f-t or c-a-r-r-y smoothly. Never hold your breath when load handling, *but breathe freely*. BEND KNEES RATHER THAN YOUR SPINE. Your back should never look like a question mark "?" but instead

should emulate an exclamation point "!" or a slash "/" or a paren-
thesis ")"—as upright as possible.

LIFTING FROM THE GROUND

Bend knees, crouching. Pull load—say a heavy rock—onto your
toes. This allows fingers to slide underneath. Lift rock onto knees,
sliding forearms underneath. Stand up, back as straight as possible,
legs doing the work, lifting rock to chest. Curl fingers at far side of
rock.

CARRYING

Can be done as you stand now: rock at chest height, back straight.
Alternative ways of carrying (depending on shape and type of load)
are:

(a) On a shoulder. Keep changing sides to avoid straining.
(b) On hip. Rather cumbersome method. Useful when load too heavy
    to be lifted to shoulder.
(c) At pelvis level. Both arms straight down. Best if fingers can
    interlock below load. Carry loads only short distances this way.

MANEUVERING

Lifting and carrying long heavy loads like logs, posts, bouncing
cars out of ditch (see *TOO SLOW*), pieces of furniture.

Lifting

1. Use lifting principles. Grip one end of long object at best point (bumpers on car/near ground under log/under edge of sideboard). Bend knees, and keep back as straight as possible.
2. Keep lifting, then relaxing, to bounce cars.
3. Lift and walk crabwise with log, say, if on your own. Then lower that end (carefully, bending knees) and go to other end. Lift and carry this forward past the far end. Then lower and repeat with the other end.
4. Two men can maneuver a long object like this . . . each takes an end and crouches, hands low, at best gripping position. One gives commands—*Ready. Lift!* They lift together and walk crabwise rather than backwards or forwards.
5. Unwieldy rocks can be maneuvered by lifting to one edge, then rolling (while you balance rock upright) for a few feet under own momentum. Take care it doesn't land on your toes.

Pushing

PUSHING

Drive from your legs. Arms can be outstretched with elbows locked or completely bent. Back or shoulder against the object is probably best position.

(a) Place back to object, legs at 45 degrees to the ground. Bend knees dig heels into ground, then straighten legs. Repeat.
(b) Face object and push with straight arms. These together with your body and legs should be in as straight a line as possible. Lock elbows. Don't push upwards, but rather horizontally and forward. Steer the object by the *push from your legs* and angle of your shoulders and back.
(c) Bend both legs and press shoulder against object. Arms should be completely bent, but hands grip so that when you straighten legs the object moves forward (and upward at your end). Useful for object like crate which needs raising to swivel or slide into position.

SOLO FIRST AID

Fantastic self-first-aid has been done by lone survivors. American pilot hacked off leg while swinging from parachute caught in jungle canopy. Trapper used hunting knife to cut/saw/sear gangrenous leg. Both survived.

People have always survived brutal surgery. British sailors once had legs amputated and stumps sealed with pitch. Kit Carson took off a companion's arm with wagon bolt, razor and saw—searing stump with hot iron.

Women have given birth on the spot—alone. Men have dragged smashed limbs/skulls/bodies for miles . . . all should give you hope if ever similarly disabled.

If on your own when injured, but still conscious and able to move and think, you *may* be able to carry out the first-aid principles, explained later, relevant to each section (like childbirth in *TOO CROWDED*)—or enough of them to pull through.

But one factor that could be fatal is present in ALL first-aid situations—and the more you are aware of it the more you may be able to combat it . . .

SHOCK

Many people have died after injury because of untreated shock. Shock of the accident weakens the body. It lowers your vital activities. Shock increases under pain/exposure/exhaustion. It must always be treated in ALL survival situations.

TREATMENT

Act immediately—unless some more pressing need like severe bleeding. Or, if treating someone else, they stop breathing.
1. FIND SHELTER FROM RAIN/WIND/SNOW (see *TOO COLD*).
2. LIE DOWN COMFORTABLY AND SLIGHTLY RAISE FEET.
3. LOOSEN TIGHT CLOTHING WITHOUT CHILLING.
4. RELIEVE PAIN IF POSSIBLE AND TREAT INJURIES.
5. GET WARM WITH EXTRA CLOTHING/COVERING, BUT DON'T MAKE VICTIM HOT ENOUGH TO CAUSE SWEATING—DON'T OVERHEAT.
6. DRINK HOT, SWEET LIQUIDS—UNLESS INTERNAL BLEEDING SUSPECTED (see *TOO CROWDED*).
   And if you are treating someone else for shock:
7. REASSURE PATIENT.
8. AVOID NOISE AND PANIC.

GETTING A DOCTOR

A telephone operator will always be able to help you with a list of available doctors, whether you are in roadside telephone booth/strange town/home (when no answer from your own doctor's number).

A hotel proprietor will contact a doctor for you.

If no telephone near, say after road crash, stop someone passing and ask them to phone immediately.

When phoning always say where you are as exactly as possible, e.g., give nearest town/city/village and any landmarks. Say also what help is needed—how many need it.

2: TOO CROWDED

Two is a crowd when one is kicking/goring/biting the other. Suffused with pain, rage, hate and fear, your chances of surviving human or animal attack are unpredictable.

Crushed in crazed football crowd, throttled in emergency-exit stampede or trampled in rush for lifeboats—mob force is as lethal as a charge of elephants/wolves/sharks. And much more likely.

What can someone unarmed and unversed in self-defense do when things get too crowded? So different is each individual, so varied are circumstances, the only hard and fast rule is hard and fast action when it comes to the crunch.

RECOGNIZE DANGER

Escalating panic on jammed escalator; screams in discotheque; footsteps following you; dancehall punch-up. None of these—or any other trouble—need affect you *directly*. But be near them and you could be involved.

The human body knowing itself in danger is much stronger than one which doesn't (despite escapes in crises by the drunk/sleeping/unconscious). Aware in time and body pumps adrenalin into bloodstream as a tone booster/muscle accelerator/blood-vessel constrictor. It can make all the difference between death and survival.

When trouble flares steel yourself. Expect it to spread and involve you. Hairs standing on back of neck = adrenalin at work. Take action.

PREPAREDNESS

1. FIGHT DOWN PANIC.
2. AVOID GETTING INVOLVED IF AT ALL POSSIBLE.
3. LOOK FOR AN ESCAPE ROUTE WELL IN ADVANCE.
4. TRY TO SIDESTEP TROUBLE WHEN FACE TO FACE.
5. WHEN TROUBLE IS HEAD-ON—RESIST WITH EVERYTHING.

SELF-PRESERVATION

CRUSHED IN CROWD

Aim to ride like buoy in rough sea where tide is extremely powerful. To go under means drowning from suffocation and trampling. Brace like a powerful spring (as shown).

Buoy position in crowd

1. TAKE DEEP BREATH.
2. TENSE BICEPS/SHOULDERS/BACK AGAINST PRESSURE.
3. BUNCH ARMS IN FRONT OF STOMACH—POSSIBLY SHIELDING CHILD WITHIN.
4. LIFT BOTH FEET OFF GROUND SO THEY ARE NOT TRAMPLED ON.
5. KEEP MOVING WHEREVER POSSIBLE.

At first signs of crowd-surge squirm away from anything solid like wall, barrier or pillar. Undo shirt collar and loosen tie.

In hysterical/swaying/terrified crowd this is all you can do. Note: Most vulnerable position of all is to be caught with hands in pockets. Neither should you clasp hands with interlocked fingers in front of body.

Where crowd is limited—too many trying to get out of emergency exit, say—try to calm panic by shouting humorous understatements.

WOMAN BEING FOLLOWED

At sign of persistent footsteps behind . . .

1. WALK FASTER.

If footsteps still follow . . .

2. RUN.

If footsteps follow running . . .

3. SCREAM.

If attacked give your resistance everything.

Screaming is often sufficient deterrent. But if not, fight like hell. The object is to stay alive, so don't use half measures.

Think ahead when followed and choose some weapon to have in hand if grabbed, from whole arsenal you carry—from high heels to hat pins.

(a) Umbrella stabbed forward.

(b) Comb with teeth dragged across *underneath* nose.

(c) Matchbox held protruding from thumb side of fist—struck hard on assailant's temples.

(d) Nail file/hairpins/safety pins/fingernails/ballpoint pens/hairbrush handle—all useful jabbers and gougers.

(e) Key ring held in palm with keys sticking through slits between fingers.

(f) Face powder blown or hair spray sprayed into attacker's eyes.

(g) Coins slipped between fingers of clenched fist in advance.

(h) Handbag with hand and wrist slipped through strap ready to swing as a club or wield stiletto heel like a battle-axe.

If approached suddenly by man, and no time for running—TALK. And in meantime prepare defenses as above (looping hand through handbag strap etc.).

BREAKING GRIPS

Use everything: Belt knee hard into testicles; smash with foot under attacker's knee, drag foot down shin and stamp on instep of attacker's foot. Kick under kneecap.

Close-range kick with knee is best as it is harder for the protagonist to grab and pull you off-balance. But if you do kick from a distance (say against knife/bottle/razor attack), don't use orthodox football-type kick which can be seen coming for miles. Do it this way:

1. LIFT KNEE UP INTO YOUR STOMACH.
2. LEAN BACK.
3. SHOOT LEG OUT HORIZONTALLY TURNING FOOT SIDEWAYS.
4. PULL FOOT BACK INSTANTLY AFTER CONNECTING.

Ram with point of elbow; butt with head if in range; pry off fingers by wrenching them backwards—especially the little fingers; escape through the attacker's thumbs (see later); use persistent pressure with edge of little finger (palm flat, fingers together, thumb flexed outwards) under assailant's nose to break fierce grip (not necessarily on you). Dig thumbnail into cuticles of attacker's fingers.

Stick fingers into attacker's eyes (first and little fingers, or first and third fingers, of one hand make useful jabbing fork spaced just right for most eyeballs).

Distract attention INSTANTLY when attacked. Handkerchief/ ashtray contents/spit can be aimed at attacker's face followed up by your own attack. Or escape.

But be QUICK about it.

ARM FROM BEHIND THROTTLING YOU. If right arm is being used then attacker's right foot will probably be forward and just behind yours (and vice versa if left arm is used). Stamp hard on instep with heel.

FINGERS STRANGLING YOU FROM BEHIND. Grab any of fingers and bend them backwards, then whip hands sideways away from your head.

STRANGLED FROM THE FRONT.

(a) Grab any finger/fingers and bend/twist/wrench QUICKLY backwards, shoving his hands far apart, or

(b) Bring both of your arms (closed together) up between opponent's hands viciously and moving outward to cleave the grip. Note: Do a shin-grinding and instep-stamping follow-up—one variation of retaliation.

BEAR-HUGGED FROM FRONT. Slap an arm up over outside one of attacker's arms. QUICKLY cup his chin and snap his head back. Chuck knee up hard and stamp on instep when all else fails.

Breaking stranglehold

BODY-HUGGED FROM BEHIND. Pry his fingers back INSTANTLY, before grip becomes concrete. Butting backwards with head can work if upper arms pinned—then grab for attacker's fingers (if set in con-solidated grip try screwing knuckles into back of hand).

PUSHED IN CHEST. Press both hands on top of hand pushing you, lean forward, step backwards and force down with bottom edges of your hands to lever him down. Very effective.

WRISTS (AND LOWER ARMS) GRIPPED. Escape through the thumbs which are weakest part (as shown). If your hands held up to protect face and wrists grabbed—swing both arms down and outward im-mediately, and break his grip at the thumbs.

If your hands low and wrists or forearms gripped, then instantly wrench arms up and outward, again pressuring opponent's thumbs.

But if two hands are gripping one of your wrists whip up your other hand between attacker's arms, close over fist of the imprisoned hand and wrench either up or down (and toward attacker) depending whether your wrist being gripped is high or low.

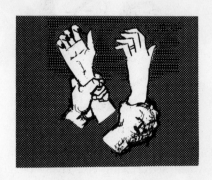

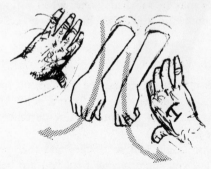

Escaping through thumbs

Or, if circumstances allow, just hit attacker with other fist in face/ solar plexus/stomach.

BEING BUTTED/KICKED/PUNCHED. Try to sway/duck/dodge with body movement first . . . as trunk movement much quicker than arm reaction. Things happen so fast you are virtually defenseless, but:

(a) When lapels grabbed be ready for being butted in face by on-coming head. Your only defense is to get in first by butting forward hard so top of your head hits opponent on bridge of nose— hard.

(b) When lying on ground and being kicked try to keep rolling, shielding parts being kicked with arms. BUT always protect head as priority. Clasp base of skull with both hands, bring wrists across ears and side of head and press elbows together. Bring knees up, crossing ankles to save genitals.

Kidney and head protection

In all attacks it pays to shout/gasp/yell more than you need: Feign pain. Especially when at receiving end (lying on ground and being kicked). Attacker may be satisfied sooner when you appear in agony.

Shout when attacking too. Expelling air makes you stronger/excited/intimidates.

WHEN FACING WEAPON

If no space to maneuver, no escape avenue, no inclination to get out—try to take weapon away (apart from a gun where you have to play it by ear—talk/divert attention if circumstances favorable/but usually acquiesce).

Person with gun could feel so upper-hand that he is careless. If absolutely essential you must *escape* (say you are being herded into truck preparatory to be being thrown into the Mississippi in a sack), think of a rush attack. The corny old cowboy film trick of glancing over gunman's shoulder can still help you there. Do it subtly. Look of dawning recognition quickly stifled might make your captor start to look around. When shot at from a distance, chuck yourself flat.

But never rush a knife . . .

Keep attacker at distance. Use chair/spade/ice axe—anything solid and handy. Jab/stab/prod in defense rather than make roundhouse swings. Make sure assailant doesn't grab your defensive gear with his free hand.

Note how knife is held.

(a) If it is going to be thrown at you, attacker will usually have to change grips on it which gives you a moment's warning.

(b) Beware knife held underarm which is stabbed upwards and can slip through ribs easily and can mean expertise in attacker.

(c) Knife stabbed down at you could be sign that assailant isn't real knife fighter (though not necessarily so) as harder for knife to enter ribs from above.

Ways of removing weapon differ tremendously. Three quick methods are shown which work so long as knife wrist can be caught quickly enough—the hard part.

Note: When all else fails—especially in drunken bottle-brawls—lash foot into genitals, but don't hesitate once you decide to kick.

Such a kick gives you more reach than the man with the weapon—especially as your body leans back as counterbalance. Aim hard at the knee. It can prove *very* effective.

Diagrams show the holds. When knife is coming upwards in attacker's right hand, try to grab that wrist with your right hand and pull his arm across your body. At same time twist your body sharply to right so his elbow lies across your body. Belt your left arm across his chest to divorce him from knife (this can also snap his arm).

Knife striking down in attacker's right hand: Try to catch that wrist with your left hand, then slot your right hand under his elbow and lock it on your *own* wrist. Force his arm back until he is forced to drop weapon (or have his arm broken).

Underarm-knife-attack defense

Another way is to catch knife wrist with both hands (overhand grip) twist your trunk hard left, duck under attacker's armpit, yanking hard to break his knife-hold.

Combating overarm knifing

Twisting to break knife grip

Note: Champagne cork incorrectly released *is* a missile—with a velocity of 30 mph and the strength of a mine or quarry blast. It is no joke to those blinded by flying cork (as many have been).

Tilt bottle to cut down air space and wet cork. Cover bottle neck and cork with a napkin while undoing wire. Ease cork off with a *sigh*, not a bang. Point bottle away from faces (including yours).

WHILE THEY ARE TYING YOU UP

Whether to foil natives strapping you to a stake or assailant who breaks into house while you are watching TV and binds you to a chair . . . knowing basic escapology is a must (you don't have to be a Houdini to get away). So when they start binding you . . .

1. ARMS TO BODY. Take deep breath. Pull shoulders back. Flex arms against the bonds. Try to fold arms by simulating pain under the armpits so crossing arms while pretending to rub sore parts—then take up as much slack as possible with second finger

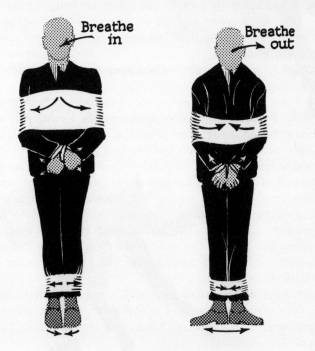

Bracing against bonds

(longest) while binder is unsighted on the blind side and/or underneath armpits.

Let breath out, shoulders slump forward and arms press into body—and bonds should slacken as you go smaller.

2. WRISTS AND HANDS. Brace these against the bonds, arched slightly. When keeping wrists apart press on fingertips and vice versa. PUSH against bonds, especially at point where they are being bound, using this counter pressure.

Free by relaxing hands and wrists and working until slack can ride over palms and fingertips—helped by long second fingers which can feed loose loops over hands. Use teeth if knots in suitable position. Or work knot loose on some pointed projection.

3. LEGS AND ANKLES. Flex thighs, knees, calves and ankles against the bonds. When bound at ankles, brace shoe toes and knees together, forcing ankles apart. Keep feet (at toes) together and arch legs apart when thighs and calves are being bound.

Free by relaxing legs. It is possible to free ankles, even though wrists still tied, if feet curled up behind and knot is in suitable place.

4. GAG. Try to free by rubbing face against wall, piece of furniture, anything projecting.

5. IF THEY TIE YOU TO TREES, FENCE POST, CHAIR. Same principles apply. Brace where possible against bonds, forcing part of body being bound away from object no matter how slightly by pressure against object elsewhere—e.g., being bound by shoulders to tree force back away from tree by pressing with calves at bottom of tree. Note: Irregular surfaces like trees present good chances of escape as working bonds towards any depressions in tree means more slack.

Remember . . . even ½-inch slack in bonds can mean escape using these principles. Usually you can obtain more by determining your captors shall not do exactly as they want with you and bracing against the rope/electric cord/wire.

A long rope bound round and round you gives better chance of escape than several short ropes at different points—ankles, wrists, chest and arms. When you see bonds overlapping realize you have chance of working slack.

Another resort: *Fray* bonds on any sharp projection—rope is easier to saw through than cord.

POTENTIAL ATTACKERS

BURGLAR

Don't have a go unless in self-defense. He may be violent. Try to get to phone. Ring police as soon as you know you are robbed. Burglars usually look for an easy touch—not trouble.

HITCHHIKER WHO PULLS WEAPON

Golden rule is: Never pick up hitchhikers.

If you do and worst happens try to do *something*—what depends on circumstances. If you haven't chance to act quickly when customer turns nasty, acquiesce and drive on. But be thinking of best action. Remember drivers who did nothing and were left shot or stabbed at the wheel. And you do have whip hand as driver.

Things that have worked:

(a) Managing to pass on SOS at filling station—possibly when gunman has "hostage" (your front-seat passenger) but lets you get out.

(b) Crossing double white lines in front of police car; flashing lights at patrol car; or misbehaving any way you can think of.

(c) Surreptitiously pulling out choke, explaining jerky engine as serious gas pump/carburetor/electrical trouble which needs attention—and once out of car RUN. (If assailant has gun run in zigzags to nearest cover.)

(d) Feigning sickness: diabetic insulin shortage/heart trouble/appendicitis while clutching body/slump over wheel/pull onto side. Then either overpower and thump or get out and run.

Remember here your elbow is strongest weapon available when struck into passenger's floating ribs (just above waist). Some other pretext may give you opening to strike thus—say extending arm as if to adjust choke/ashtray/wipe windshield.

(e) With front seat hitchhiker holding gun/knife/razor on you, consider stopping very, very abruptly if you are wearing seat belt and he is not. And eject him onto dashboard/windshield.

(f) If a good-enough driver, give unwanted passenger very fast drive so he knows that to kill or injure you while at wheel will mean horrifying crash.

If driving with valuable load and stopped by someone who suggests you get out to attend to flat tire/unsafe load/lights out/an accident ahead—don't leave your vehicle. Drive on until sure you are safe then check.

Waved down by police (and with valuable load) don't leave vehicle if asked—but offer to drive to nearest police station. Bogus police and identification cards hard to detect from real thing at night.

DRIVER WHO KIDNAPS HITCHHIKER

Put on vomiting act all over car interior. You may manage real thing if you stick two fingers down your throat. If car stops get out and run.

See also *TOO FAST* (when driver is drunk, suicidal).

PEEPING TOM

Don't attack—he might be in shouting distance of other kinky characters who "patrol" lovers' lanes/parks/turn-offs after closing time.

If in car parked in field/lane/woods and face looms at window— stay inside. Doors should be locked and windows wound up. Don't open window to anyone who taps on it—it could admit a gun.

Fact the spyer has been seen is enough usually to make him sheer off. In any case—drive off yourself.

Don't rush into the attack in face of such complete unknown.

FIGHTING DRUNK

Humor.

If involved in brawl, drunks can offer astoundingly strong grip. Hit hard in stomach and this may make him sick.

MADMAN

Humor (again can have three times the strength of normal person).

FURIOUS DRIVER

Avoid being pulled from your car seat and battered by motorist/ truck driver/cabbie who is incensed at way you cut in front of him and catches you at traffic lights. Lock doors and refuse to get out. Blow horn.

If driving door is forced open, back out through other front door. Or slam door shut on his wrist.

Or jump out towards complainant—fast. Don't sit there as sitting target for a punch in the nose. Or possibly worse.

Talking alone can often get you out of this spot—but be ready.

MOB

Can vary from a small crowd angered by your hitting pedestrian/ car/pushcart with your vehicle while on vacation to lynching party out for blood.

Get away—escape in time.

If not, back to the wall.

If you can dispatch the first assailant to lay hands on you summarily enough, the others MAY have second thoughts about coming to grips with you.

DROWNING PERSON

Keep well away as drowning people have strong fighting instinct (see *TOO WET*). Break holds as above if grabbed by drowner (say following shipwreck).

NATIVES

If attacked take cover. Avoid fighting back unless poisoned darts (you suspect) are showering at you. And then fire *above* heads. Killing primitive tribesman will really precipitate things.

When you feel you are being watched in jungle, stand in any clearing, show yourself empty-handed in all directions. If still not sure, leave gifts in obvious place and come back to check if still there.

On meeting natives . . . show yourself unarmed by holding out arms and hands. Use sign language to show your needs, and you may be taken to village.

(a) Play it by ear. Take things slowly. Show yourself friendly/well-intentioned/not scared. Smile.

(b) Aim to see headman. Ask him for any help you need. Sign language will get through. Don't demand. Give gifts.

(c) Don't be too generous in handing out possessions/coins (not paper money)/food as payment. It is unwise to overpay. Be fair —try to win their confidence. Keep promises.

(d) Respect customs—and native homes/*women*/possessions. If you don't leave them alone, expect the worst. Survival when tribesmen are not sure about you is very much a case of doing as you would be done by.

(e) Mix. Join in. Be prepared to become butt of their humor. Try to learn their tongue. Don't keep repeating faux pas which are obviously causing consternation.

(f) Learn what you can of locale, food and water supplies. Also whereabouts of hostile natives, anything that can help.

(g) Watch your possessions aren't pinched. Avoid living in native shelters (you could catch disease) if at all possible, but build your own, possibly with native help. Boil your water, prepare your own food—but don't make your segregation (for health reasons) obvious.

CREATURES FROM OUTER SPACE
(STEPPING FROM FLYING SAUCER)

Avoid rapid forceful movement.
Use no shrill sounds.
Breathe quietly.
Avoid giving a direct menacing gaze.

ANIMAL HAZARDS

Animal attack is unpredictable.

You can expect it when hunting/trapping/filming big game, but mostly fear lies *in the mind* of survivor in wilderness country. You could well escape without ever seeing a dangerous animal, and discover those you do avoid you.

Animal kingdom *does* offer real danger, however—when cornered/surprised/with young. Some need no provocation.

Animal hazard is not only present in jungle, but in many places—parks/reservations/fields/mountains/streets/sea.

BULLS

Keep your eye on the bull. Biggest cause of fatalities and injuries is carelessness/familiarity/contempt. Bulls are completely unpredictable.

If you *have* to go in field with bull, keep to edges. Otherwise detour outside the field—some bulls may take no notice of intruders some of the time, then attack. They can run and swerve faster than humans. Remember—maddened cows can charge, too.

Ways to evade . . .

(a) Fling taken-off coat (or any hand-held object) into bull's path. There is a good chance the bull will pause to investigate decoy with horn before resuming chase, which gives you time to take another garment off as you run. Keep stripping.

(Diagram showing this is optimistic in amount of ground escaper gains, but shows the principle and makes the point: Farmers knowing this technique go into bull's field armed with sack.)

Bull evasion

(b) Bulls tend to go for any bright colors—not necessarily red. Subdue anything bright as best you can.

(c) Bulls don't take to water easily—another escape avenue: river/lake outlet/canal.

(d) If with family (inconceivable if you have not been careless), draw off bull while women and children run in different directions—by flinging coat. Even then no knowing what bull will do and whom he will chase.

(e) If thrown by bull only way to hurt him is by grasping the nose ring (if there is one) and hanging on with fingers.

(f) Another survival method that has worked: Feign death if you have already survived being thrown/gored/knelt on.

DOGS

Ordinary village dog in other countries is often dangerous. Semi-starved and savage, its bite can be fatal (if dog has rabies). Signs—glazed eyes/foaming mouth/staggering.

Stone them to keep at bay if they attack you.

With other big dogs try the following deterrents, in this order:

(a) Hit on nose HARD and FAST.

(b) Brace forearm in front of you, offering it to dog. When seized jam it to back of jaws and instantly bring over your other arm (palm flexed and facing floor) so bony edge of forearm forces into back of dog's neck as you force the head backwards and over the arm with quick jerk. Rolling action.

WOLVES

Wolves are only *related* to dogs. Spinal anatomy is similar, but wolf has *protective* ruff and its spinal (cervical) vertebrae are thickly

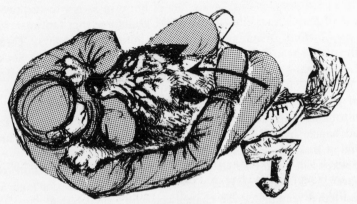

Wolf fight

encased in neck muscle. Vulnerable parts: nose, lower ribs at side. Wolves are tearers, pack hunters usually, and hunters of *weak* victims, going after limbs. If attacked by a wolf:

1. Chop it on *nose*.
2. Slam arm to back of jaws.
3. Go down with it, clutching back in crossed legs.
4. Squeeze like hell with legs and cause a reflex back-squirm, then try jerking hand on neck.

BEARS

A hazard all over world (from Arctic to Yellowstone Park). Don't encourage "tame" bears to approach you, with food/posed-photographs-with-people-included/fooling about. They can maul without warning. Observe warning notices in such areas.

Marauding polar bear prowling around forced camp should be shot: hard and dangerous to kill, yet relentless in its curiosity. Aim shots for neck/heart/throat/just behind shoulder. One marksman on own very vulnerable.

TIGERS

All big cats can either sheer away or attack. Unarmed survivors who have been face to face with tigers/leopards/lions have used various methods: freezing still; staring back hard; yelling, screaming.

SNAKES

In snake-prone country make lots of noise so as not to surprise— cause of most snake bites. Wear boots. Reinforce thin footwear with layers of cloth. Wind around ankles (but not too tight). Thrash with stick ahead when stepping over logs/rocks/thickets. Snakes are nocturnal—take flashlight and thick stick at night. Don't sleep on ground. Watch where you put bare hands.

If bitten, try to kill snake (with rock/stick/gun)—if you or companions have presence of mind in ensuing alarm. When sure it is dead handle by tail and take to doctor/hospital/sick bay in camp (kind of snake means venom can be identified).

Snakes will usually avoid you. Only 200 are fatally poisonous out of over 2,000 different kinds. Even poisonous snakes don't always inject lethal venom. A good chance you won't die if bitten.

See later for treatment.

SPIDERS

Avoid by not rooting/groping/feeling under rocks, logs and in holes with your hands in potential spider country—whether in home-docked banana boat or abroad.

Black widow (with reddish, hourglass marking underneath) has most dangerous nerve poison, which can kill. Tarantula is relatively harmless by comparison. Spiders don't often kill—but inflict pain.

Hairy spiders cause intense skin irritation if they touch you.

SCORPIONS

Be wary. They lie in dark places: Don't disturb with bare hands when working among tree trunks/logs/rocks/sand. Knock shoes/socks/clothing before dressing. Check bedding before you lie on it.

Poison affects nerve system, makes you vomit and can kill—especially children. Smaller scorpions are more potent than big ones. The poison glands are in tail and big claws.

CENTIPEDES

Check clothing and bedding in hot climates. Nocturnal. If you feel one crawling over you in night—let it. Don't attempt to brush off. Very painful sting.

INSECTS

Disease (like malaria and yellow fever from mosquitoes) is biggest fatality risk. Cover up at all costs against swarms of flies.

(a) Cover face/extremities/upper body with mud.

(b) Improvise wide-brimmed hat.

(c) Improvise head net from shirt/undershirt/T-shirt (sleeves pulled up through buttoned-up neckhole) worn around and over head and tucked into collar.

(d) Wear two layers of clothing where possible. Tuck trousers into socks/boots/puttees (made from cloth wound round and round spirally upwards from ankle to knees). Tie off bottom of trousers inside footgear with laces/string/vines. Tuck sleeves into gloves (makeshift ones: socks).

(e) Keep clothes on at night. Improvise mosquito net around bedding from any cloth.

(f) Use first-aid ointment/repellent/antimalaria tablets if available.

Pitching camp on *right* site is important. Steer clear of (1) swamps/pools/bogs; (2) low-lying, damp and calm land; (3) sheltered site. Instead chose high windy situation where possible.

Insect-proof shelter as tightly as materials allow—say with parachute canopy, or clothing. Cigarette smoke is a deterrent inside, but smoky fire better.

Light healthy fire outside, then add damp foliage/ferns/moss until smoking heavily. A smaller section of this is carried into back of shelter. Fan smoke (along with flies) back out through door.

ANTS

Avoid anthills and ant paths. Beware when climbing tropical trees as ants that bite live high as well as at ground level. Look where you sit and sleep. Don't scatter food remains around—bury them.

Faced with remorseless march of ant army—just move your gear out of the path which will keep in a straight line (but do it in time).

TICKS, LEECHES, FLEAS

Strip off clothes often—especially in grassy areas. You may find ticks/leeches/bed bugs—among others. Examine each other. Ticks can be removed by brushing/flicking/tapping. But if head is attached under skin, relax its grip with iodine/alcohol/lit-cigarette-held-near. Don't pull body, or head remains in and festers.

Leeches respond to flicking/salt/cigarette end (they will get through any clothing). Don't *pull* if already attached to you.

Fleas burrowing under toenails (or skin) to lay eggs may generally be removed with fire-sterilized knife/needle/pricker. And iodine applied.

There are many other parasites which can burrow below skin, fleas which can bite and insects which can fill you with disease.

BEES, WASPS, HORNETS

If you disturb a nest (usually 10 to 30 feet up trees) and you are some yards away sit tight for several minutes, then crawl away (wasps chase moving targets). If attacked run through thickest undergrowth or take to water.

IN ALL PEST-PRONE AREAS

(a) Keep clothes on as barrier (with layers tucked in).

(b) Keep clothing dry as possible, clean and mended. Especially socks and stockings. Wash a lot.

(c) Never walk barefooted.

(d) If you fall into tropical water, no matter how fresh-looking, act: Wring clothing; drain shoes; towel down all over; change into dry clothes if possible.

(e) Keep out of water unless forced to wade, as tremendous variety of attackers from water-borne, skin-burrowing worms to sting rays; jellyfish to barracuda; water snakes to electric eels; Portuguese Man-of-War to coral-reef stingers.

CROCODILES AND ALLIGATORS

They can lie with eyes just above water like logs. Or on banks.

Beware when wading across rivers, swimming or rafting across bays and estuaries in tropics. Don't thrash/splash/shout. Skirt well clear of any such infested water. If attacked get to side FAST. Check thoroughly first before entering any deep water. Don't trust method of throwing stones to scare off crocodiles.

If you do confront one at close quarters—stay vertical. Hands and arms rigid at sides, feet sunk in mud/silt/earth gives you a slightly better chance.

SHARKS

Keep quiet in raft. Paddle away from blood/vomit/fish remnants/ excrement floating on water. Avoid fishing near sharks. Wear dark clothing if possible and cover bare limbs as white flash can attract them.

Don't jump overboard to swim from small boats without checking all around and underneath. Stay near boat. Avoid dangling hands or feet over side. Sharks come scavenging around craft without warning. If investigated be ready for craft to be nudged/scraped/bumped by shark. Avoid flashing bright objects to attract them even more. Keep quiet. Chances are they might lose interest if no apparent chance of food and swim on.

When attacked by shark and you are on raft: All face out back to back (tie yourselves together if rough sea) and kick out at shark; use knife in gills or eyes; jab snout/gills/eye with oar by prodding/ stabbing/jabbing—not swinging.

If anyone dies throw body over at night and paddle away fast. Pull anyone injured into raft and treat for bleeding (see later) and shock (see *TOO LONELY*).

Gunshot can scare.

Use shark repellent if available.

Swimmers in shark-infested water should use regular smooth strokes. Panicky splashing movements attract the big fish. Also—stay clear of large schools of fish (another shark attraction).

Survivors in water without raft facing shark (or any dangerous fish like barracuda or swordfish) should form a circle facing outward and beat the water with powerful regular strokes. Float if you see triangular fin and shark doesn't seem to have spotted you.

Swimmer can try these measures when single shark attacks.

(a) Don't turn and flee but face and swim to one side as he comes in.

(b) Suddenly swim *at* shark.

(c) At close quarters—try kicking/punching/handing off.

(d) Scream underwater.

(e) Slap surface water with hands.

(f) If armed—stab gills or eye.

CROWD HAZARDS

Crowd risks run gamut from apoplectic argument which results in heart attack to bite of snake/punch of fist/kick of boot. Or emergency birth of baby.

SHOCK

ALWAYS treat—this goes for all hazards. (See *TOO LONELY*.)

BLEEDING

Priority hazard of all—even to nonbreathing (see *TOO WET*).

Act FAST when someone is losing lifeblood.

A little blood looks a lot. But blood is antiseptic and will usually clot itself—so long as flow is slowed. Can take a few seconds to over ten minutes.

1. PRESS DIRECTLY WITH FINGERS (UNLESS STEEL/ ROCK/WOOD EMBEDDED).
2. PRESS ON PAD (HANDKERCHIEF) TO MAKE BLOOD STOP OR OOZE.
3. RAISE BLEEDING PART OF BODY.

4. GET TO DOCTOR/HOSPITAL FAST.

Don't wash wound
Don't peel off blood clot
Don't use tourniquet or bandage too tightly
Don't take off pad—add more on top if bleeding through.

Clean pad is not essential though preferable. Don't mess around looking for hygienic one. Use handiest to check spurting blood.

Forget about looking for special pressure points (easily forgotten in crisis). Pinch wound edges together with fingers. Keep pressing no matter how exhausted/bloody/scared stiff you are.

Remember: Raising a bleeding limb will force blood to run uphill and slow down bleeding rate. Do that.

BLEEDING INSIDE VICTIM

Happens in violent accidents—falling/crashing/crushing.

Injured is cold/clammy/pale. Pulse is weak and faint. Pain. Restlessness. Eyesight goes dim. Thirst grows. Frothy, red or coffee-colored blood is spewed up sometimes. Bowel movement can look like tar or be stained crimson.

Play safe. Don't give drinks (wet lips with moistened cloth). Move as little as possible. Get medical aid.

UNCONSCIOUSNESS

Test by touching eyeball gently—a blink means injured is conscious.

Never shout/shake/pummel. Don't try to force down fluids (and never try to give alcohol). If back does not appear broken (see *TOO FAST*) . . .

1. TURN BODY AND HEAD TO ONE SIDE.
2. CLEAR MOUTH OF DENTURES/VOMIT/DIRT AND CHECK BREATHING.
3. LOOK FOR BLEEDING AND STOP.
4. LOOSEN CLOTHING AND TREAT FOR INJURIES.
5. SEARCH POCKETS FOR IDENTITY—AND NOTICE OF DIABETES ETC.

Get stretcher/medical help/ambulance.

FRACTURED BONES

Can range from break under unbroken skin to smashed bone ends rammed into each other. Sometimes bones stick into view, sometimes into internal organs.

Signs (if not obvious): PAIN, shock, power loss in limb. Swelling (compare one leg, say, with the other for size).

Never—unless going to be in wilds for ages—try to fix fracture back into place. Survivors in way-out situations have tractioned breaks on their own (like single man who hooks ankle of broken leg into fork of tree and pulls to reset leg straight). Normal situations need opposite of this treatment.

LEAVE BROKEN BONES ALONE AS MUCH AS POSSIBLE UNTIL THEY CAN BE PROPERLY TREATED BY DOCTOR OR HOSPITAL.

More danger from doing too much than too little.

ELIMINATE PAIN: This is best you can do. If your treatment does this, no matter how little or how rough and ready, you are doing a good job. Elevate limb if possible—as fracture nearly always bleeds inside.

If injured crying out in pain, or HAS to be moved . . . *don't* jab/prod/finger bones sticking into view. Stop bleeding. Ease limb into most comfortable position. Splint to support a break with rolled-up newspapers/magazines/sticks—anything handy. And pad softly with rags/clothes/leaves. (Never use metal in cold climate.)

Tie firmly with make-do bandages—ties/belts/cloth strips. And realize body makes best splint—arm to body, leg to leg, jaw to jaw—and so on.

Immobilizing broken limb

DON'T splint if possible. Wait for help.

Fractured skull (see later), broken spine (see *TOO FAST*), smashed pelvis . . . all asking for horrible trouble if you try moving unless absolutely necessary—and you know the score.

WOUNDS

Slit–cut–rip any clothing carefully (so it can be sewn up again if necessary). Be meticulous about NOT touching wound with fingers/ having dirty hands/rubbing muck into sore.

Sterilize tip of knife or needle with several matches before picking out foreign objects with point.

Wash around wound with soap and water (always smoothing away from edge of wound, never towards it). Don't pour iodine into the wound, though it can be used to clean surrounding skin (let it dry in air before dressing).

Swabbing wound with clean cloths and soap and water okay when surrounding edges cleaned.

BE SCRUPULOUSLY CLEAN.

When wound punctured by nail/knife/stabber squeeze wound to press out blood—and help cleanse.

Apply as clean a dressing as possible—not too tight. Doctor needed: Don't forget lockjaw risk.

DISLOCATION

Wrenched/twisted/cocked bone at joint. Unusual shape tells of dislocation. Pain/power loss/stiffness.

1. DON'T TRY TO TWIST BACK INTO PLACE.
2. SUPPORT IN MOST COMFORTABLE POSITION (PAD WHERE NECESSARY).
3. FORGET ABOUT SPLINTS.

SPRAINS

Bruised swelling after wrist or ankle has been in impact.

1. REST/IMMOBILIZE/ELEVATE.
2. APPLY WET CLOTHS.

Wrist: Make a simple sling to support arm against body.

Ankle: Wrap bandage in firm figure eight around ankle and foot.

If swelling grows, untie, rewet and retie.

CHEMICAL BURNS
(See TOO HOT.)

BLACK EYE

Apply wet cloths.

HUMAN BITE

Dangerous; warrants a doctor. Flood immediately with running water.

SNAKE BITE

Rare death. Skip those old heroics where trusty companion slashes bite site with knife and sucks out venom. Kill snake if possible—*someone.*
1. DON'T PANIC AND RUSH/FLAP/RUN AROUND.
2. TELL VICTIM TO LIE DEAD STILL.
3. APPLY FIRM BANDAGE ON HEART SIDE OF BITE (LOOSEN IT FOR ONE MINUTE EVERY HALF HOUR).
4. WASH (NOT RUB) SURFACE OF BITE WITH WATER.
5. TREAT FOR SHOCK AND GIVE NO DRINKS.
6. CARRY TO DOCTOR/HOSPITAL (WITH DEAD SNAKE IF POSSIBLE) IMMEDIATELY.

DOG BITE

1. WASH WELL WITH SOAPY WATER.
2. BUT WASH SALIVA WELL AWAY FROM WOUND.
3. COVER WITH DRY CLEAN DRESSING.
4. KEEP PART IMMOBILE (SPLINT).
Get patient to hospital.

FOX/RAT/BAT BITES

Chance of rabies from these. Get bite under running water or wash well with soap. Then dress.

ANT/MOSQUITO BITES

Ease pain with baking-soda-plus-water paste. Cover with wet cloth when swelling.

BEE/WASP STING

Try to get sting out with tweezers or by prying carefully with flame-sterilized tip of needle or knife. Run cold water over. Piece of soap comforts bee sting; vinegar or lemon, wasp sting.

When swarm has stung in mass soak in bath with baking soda stirred in (cool) or smooth mud over stings.

HEART ATTACK

Symptoms: Sudden clutching at bar/desk/side. Shortness of breath; pain in upper abdomen or chest (with pains shooting down arms or up into neck and head); coughing up pink froth (perhaps).

Doctor QUICK.

Meanwhile . . .

1. GET INJURED AS COMFORTABLE AS CAN BE (OFTEN HALF LYING DOWN).
2. LOOSEN CLOTHING.
3. COVER PATIENT (BUT DON'T OVERHEAT).
4. DON'T CARRY OR GIVE DRINK.
5. TELL TO BREATHE DEEPLY, SLOWLY, BLOWING OUT THROUGH MOUTH.

Give Kiss of Life (see *TOO WET*) if breathing stops.

CHOKING

Don't scrabble with fingers when something jams in throat—and dig it in further. Coughing often the solution. And medical help.

(a) Infant: Hold upside down by legs, and smack sharply up to six times between shoulders.

(b) Child: Lay across knee, head down, your hand under upper abdomen/chest. Ditto for infant.

(c) Adult: Bend head down or lie across table/log/rock. Same for infant.

HEAD INJURY

Violent blow (in car crash/punch-up/drunken fall) on skull could equal dizziness/coma/bleeding from mouth, ears, nose. Headache. Odd eye pupils.

Lie injured down. Cover up. Never let them struggle up and stagger about. If spine not broken (see *TOO FAST*) and face is flushed, raise head on folded jacket/coat/sweater. IF PALE DO NOT RAISE HEAD.

Turn body and head gently to one side (if no broken back suspected) so blood/mucous/vomit drains out. Fit light, clean dressing on head if bleeding (don't bind hard forcing bones into brain).

Remember—lying quietly (even if conscious) until medical help at hand is aim.

EMERGENCY CHILDBIRTH

Happens anytime. Don't panic. Not unique situation. Let nature handle it with you helping it along.

Above all . . .

1. DON'T PULL BABY OR ITS CORD OR AFTERBIRTH ATTACHED TO OTHER END OF CORD.
2. TIE CORD AS SOON AS BABY IS DELIVERED.
3. CUT CORD ONLY IF NO HELP LIKELY. IF HELP ON WAY, TIE CORD BUT LEAVE AFTERBIRTH ATTACHED.
4. KEEP BABY WARM: PLACE BETWEEN MOTHER'S LEGS.

Signs are: Uterus starting to contract within each half hour (very roughly). When pint of water pours out things really moving.

Preparation: Lie mother-to-be on something flat, and spread with clean sheet/newspapers/plastic. Have hot water on hand if possible. Wash hands carefully. Wear handkerchief over mouth when helping. No messing—be clean. Give loads of encouragement.

Pad drawer/carton/tub for baby. Boil scissors well first. Get three lengths of string each about a handspan's length (just over) for cord tying.

Put mother in best position when bulge appears and birth imminent. Knees up, back near edge of delivery table.

If bowels move wipe clean towards spine, away from birth route.

As birth happens tell mother to pant and *not* bear down. Baby's head/bottom/foot/arm could come first—don't pull, but feed it out. Only interfere if membrane is over baby's face (tear it). Or if cord is around baby's neck (ease/loop/slide it free). If head comes last and sticks pull gently three minutes after shoulders have come.

BE GENTLE. IF CORD IS MISTREATED BABY MIGHT
BLEED TO DEATH.

Lay baby (frog-slippery—don't drop) between mother's legs,
cord not stretched, head downhill. And care for it thus:

(a) Bind ankles with cloth.

(b) Hook your fingers under binding and hang upside down. Let fluids
drain from mouth and nose after opening mouth and holding
head back a bit.

(c) Wipe face and mouth very gently with clean piece of cloth.

(d) When baby cries lay on side close to mother—not face down.

(e) If no crying or gurgling/bubbling/breathing don't smack and
handle abrasively: give a very gentle Kiss of Life in about two
minutes.

Ten minutes later (approximate) afterbirth will come, mother
separating her legs and helping it out. (Note: bleeding can be
checked often by gently massaging under the navel. Keep afterbirth
intact in some container.)

If medical help some way off: Tie the cord. Do this firmly about
6 inches from baby's navel, then another knot 8 inches away. Cut
cord in between. If no bleeding after another ten minutes tie another knot 4 inches from baby's navel.

Bathe mother. Give her hot drinks. Treat for shock. *Congratu-
late.* Reassure. Keep check on breathing/pulse. Let her sleep.

3: TOO DRY

Thirst bursts through every human need. Owed water, the body is a debt collector ruthless enough to force its demented owner to drink gasoline/radiator water/sea water in an effort to exact repayment.

A raging need in hot climates, thirst is more insidious in cold: You may not feel the pangs until too late. But 4 pints of water a day are essential to keep you going *efficiently* in cool weather, and at least a gallon in hot. It is as ultimate as this.

The castaway can fight thirst by sucking a green leaf (which doesn't help physiologically) and controlling his perspiration rate (which does). But in the long run he *must* find water. And having found it, try to make it fit to drink.

STAVING OFF THIRST

SUCK SOMETHING

Try it and see. You may feel risk of swallowing hard object is too great. Choose something smooth and nonabsorbent and small: nut/pebble/leaf/gum. Prune is excellent. So is piece of raw onion.

Sucking snow or ice is not recommended (makes you more thirsty, and chills stomach). If you do, hold melted water in mouth to take off chill before swallowing. Take a little food at same time to attune stomach.

Cigarettes can help—but also dry mouth more than ever.

PACE YOURSELF

Main aims must be to sweat as little as possible. Water lost through perspiration must be replaced. In a hot climate move as if in slow motion. Your need for water rises astronomically if you are very active in the heat. Conserve precious body water with calculated action when moving about.

DON'T RUSH/PANIC/RUN

Cold weather will demand hard work (making shelter/collecting firewood/gathering ice or snow for water)—even so, try to sweat as little as possible (see *TOO COLD*).

Rest often. Sleep whenever possible. Work on rotation if jobs to be done, so some are resting while minimum number do their stint.

REGULATE CLOTHING

A hot climate calls for body cover to check sweat evaporation. Add clothes instead of subtracting them. Button up collar/sleeves/coat. Cover legs. Make headdress (see *TOO BRIGHT*). Spin out your body moisture to best effect by keeping it *in* or at second best *on* body.

Wear white in sun-bright area—white shirt over black coat say. Uncomfortable, yes, but helps to reflect heat rays that evaporate sweat.

You can only be comfortable in hot weather through losing sweat quickly—i.e., by taking your clothes off. And that, when body water is at a premium, is unaffordable luxury.

Very cold weather can mean that sweat freezes. Cut down sweat rate by loosening tight clothing/taking off clothing layers, then replacing everything when you stop (see *TOO COLD*).

KEEP COOL

Cool off in hot weather with damp pad soaked in sea water/urine/alcohol and rub face, hands, neck.

On raft/lifeboat/dinghy, soak clothes with sea water, though don't overdo this under raging sun. Unwise to jump into sea (danger of sharks and you may be too weak to get back easily).

TAKE SHADE

In hot sun you need twice as much water as in shade. So use whatever shade available—vehicle/tree/rock/dune. Shadow is the key to conserving sweat and alleviating thirst pangs which would rage more on the move. If no shelter make one from any fabric or gear you have, using lean-to or tent principles. Sleep.

In any shelter allow slits to let air circulate freely in hot atmosphere. Also sit off the ground rather than sprawl on it—it is several degrees cooler 12 inches above hot sand/soil/rock. Insulate from the ground with anything available. (Note: It is cooler *under* the surface too.)

Use the shade of night for main movement—walking and working—and get more miles per pint of water than in daytime where sun fries, frizzles, flails and terrifies. You can almost double mileage at night if you *have* to walk.

DON'T EAT

(a) Anything if water as meager as pint a day.
(b) Proteins—eggs/milk/fish/cheese—unless up to 10 pints a day as these need water for digestion. Eat fruit/sweets/crackers. Plants.

DON'T DRINK

SEA WATER

Whatever is advised here, the temptation will grow and grow and grow. The castaway, anguished with thirst, thinks that perhaps he *is* different and will be able to take salt water without harm. That perhaps there is some loophole and he'll be all right. Then vague recollections of people who survived by drinking taboo fluids come pounding in. Then what the hell . . .

And he drinks (perhaps pretending it to be accidental). And at first seems the winner. The saline refreshes, revives, assuages. It seems to last, too, until he presently is called on to sip again. And again. And again. And againandagainandagainagainagain.

His thirst, whatever before, will balloon into fiendish proportions. And quite soon, with racing pulse, sickness, enlarged tongue, blue skin, glassy eyes, deluded and deaf, he will die in delirium.

Sea water *can* be used: for cooling hot body; chilling eye compresses when you are sunblind; swilling off salt-encrusted tarpaulins/containers/decks when rain shower is due and you don't want solid salt in supply. BUT NEVER DRINK IT.

URINE

Don't drink, as salt content too high. You become thirstier. Use to make damp cooling pad in burning heat. Or to warm chilled skin in cold.

ALCOHOL

Consumption not advised. Could precipitate rash actions in survival situations.

BATTERY WATER

It might contain toxic amounts of lead.

FISH FLUIDS

Don't drink—even if you have the chance. Many have been found harmful, though there are exceptions.

GLACIER WATER

Rushing melted water from snow areas in mountains contains pounded/powdered/crushed rock. However, alternative clear-water supplies usually available on hills.

ANYTHING MILKY, SALTY, SOAPY

The exceptions (like coconut milk) are mentioned elsewhere. (See *TOO EMPTY*.)

HANDLING DRINKING WATER

EXISTING SUPPLY

Drink whenever you are thirsty. Little and often is useful to remember. Don't follow the fallacy of rationing the only pint of water into 50 egg cupfuls expecting 50 days of life. Without water in a 50-degree F. temperature you can last about ten days. With 4 pints you can do around 11—if not using energy.

By the same token in a desert temperature of 120 degrees F. you can last about two days without water. But you can still last only two days with 1 pint of water. It is the same for 3 pints. And for four. Not until you have a gallon can you hope to survive longer—and then barely another day in the terrific heat.

Drink whenever thirsty. It is the water inside you that is important. The only way to save water is to *control your sweating*.

Don't be afraid of overdrinking. You *can* consume nearly 4 pints at a time. In blistering desert conditions the body sweats this out in two hours. Besides, you use extra body water urinating/excreting/vomiting.

Drink *enough*, especially in cool climate where you may feel no need to. You still need water and, as in hot weather, it is harmful to ration body's needs when the water it craves could easily be available. You always have to make up the water debt sooner or later.

Don't drink water on the first day (unless injured) if you want to feel you are saving water. And, of course, water needs to be rationed so that everyone gets a fair share.

Remember when drinking—moisten lips, mouth and throat before swallowing. After sudden rain shower drink slowly and deeply.

Never gulp down water when parched.

ADDITIONAL SUPPLIES

When water supplies are renewed through rain/river/oasis, drink more than your fill before starting out again. Saturate your body as if it were a bank and you were filling your account to avoid being in the red for as long as possible.

If traveling in the desert take as much water as humanly possible—even possibly at the expense of other gear (see *TOO SLOW*). Carry it in covered containers.

Before starting, drink far more than you think you will need. Then en route drink often and in small doses.

The fact you were waterlogged to start with gives you a head start when you run short later.

SEARCHING FOR WATER

RAIN

Watch weather signs. Be ready for the rain. Clean dirty containers. Most materials can be waterproofed by rubbing with candle/butter/wax. Swirl boat covers/tarpaulins/sails in sea to dissolve salt crust. Some salt will still contaminate the rain water, but should not harm you.

Spread out clothes to catch rain. Remember big tree leaves/tree-trunk holes/rock depressions will do the job for you. If time dig hole in ground and line with cloth/canvas/plastic. Or oiled paper or leaves. Anything to stop rapid drainage into earth as thirsty as you.

Rain water can be diverted from leaning trees and branches by a long cloth wick (torn from any cloth) leading into a container. Dam or divert dried-up stream bed into rock basin if possible.

DEW

Can fall in great quantities in deserts and barren places.

Lay out potential dew traps: shiny surfaces like back of ground-sheet/hubcaps/airplane cowlings/tin cans.

Dig dew pit—floor it with canvas or cloth or plastic and heap in cleaned stones dug from under desert sand. Dew could collect on these and drip to floor.

Drain dew into containers. Mop dew up too. Remember it might collect on nearby plants and stones. Get up early to check.

SNOW

Don't drink when soaked by sea spray. Don't drink unless (1) no fresh water available, (2) no ice in vicinity. Snow is uneconomical to heat, takes fuel and time for small amount of water produced. And you will need 4 pints per day per person.

(Snow can be melted in hand-held snowballs—at risk of frostbite.)

Put snow into cooking pot/tin/can *bit by bit*—not in one packed lump. Compress each bit firmly. Best to have a little water already in can before you start. And when you finish drinking leave some water for next brew-up. Pack snow in tightly. Tilt can or pot on fire.

Snow from underneath surface is better and more compact for good water yield than softer surface snow.

Snow chunks can be melted on any dark cloth laid out on rock in sunshine. Lap up water puddles or pour into cooking pot. Best time for heating snow is when cooking, then you use one fire for everything.

ICE

Good water producer. Don't waste fuel though, if water available.

Distinguish *old* sea ice from *new*. And only use old ice as it is less salty. Suck it and see if it tastes salty. Old sea ice looks blue, shatters and has blunt corners. New is angular, spiky and a milky-gray color.

Iceberg ice is good but it is a risky way of getting ice (bergs can capsize even when refrozen in a pack, as ice below melts underwater faster than above).

Pools on ice floes are usually okay—in old ice. But could be salt-sprayed near water. Use common sense. And taste.

SURFACE WATER

Plants don't mean surface water. Look for other signs too. Birds twittering in desert. Birds circling over something. Use animals' trails. Game trails. Trade routes. Investigate holes (or hole) in ground—could be a well or cistern. Stick by an oasis. They are usually linked by trade routes.

MUD

Mop a cloth/handkerchief/sponge into mud, then squeeze it out.

PLANTS

Cactus-type plants are worth trying—no matter how leathery-looking. If no knife, smash/cut top off/squeeze. Try pounding on rock—you might get squelchy mush or liquid (don't drink if milky).

Don't waste energy scratching around desert scrub for water-holding roots just under surface. They do exist (perhaps radiating 50 feet out from some water "trees") but don't depend on finding them. Investigate by all means—a few feet from the "trees." Don't lose a lot of sweat over it.

Plants in jungle can contain fresh water. Try everything. Green bamboo sometimes holds thirst-quenching liquid; if split and yellow it may hold rain water; cut notch above each joint if gurgling sounds inside. Bamboo makes a good water container.

Vines excellent. Reach as high as possible up thickest vine and cut. Then lop off bottom and point end. Can be drunk straight or poured into cup (note: mouth contact with vine could lead to skin irritation). But don't drink if a milky fluid leaks out.

Green coconuts can hold two pints of excellent milk. To get into a green nut find the two "eyes" at top and drill into them with anything sharp, or smash with sharp rock just below eyes (to remove husk—exterior matting—from nut without a knife, sharpen top of a strong stake stuck upright in the ground into "axe" edge. Shove nut down on this so stake edge bites between fibers—and keep twisting).

Climbing the palm trees (see *TOO LOW*).

UNDERGROUND

Don't waste energy in a fruitless search for water that *might* be underground in hot climates unless there is some positive encouragement to go on. If you are a water diviner, fair enough. If not, save your sweat and energy. Never dig wildly at random.

The following signs in the earth's crust may mean chance of water, especially if stained, damp, moist.

(a) Caves—in limestone country (see *TOO LOW/TOO HIGH*). Cracks in rock. Springs. Moist places. Stains.

(b) Cliffs—look at base of limestone faces. In lava country, cliffs looking like organ-pipe columns might seep water.

(c) Valleys may contain springs/streams/seepages in all kinds of instances—like valley crossing lava band, or gorge in sandstone leaking water at sides.

(d) Hillsides first give you a high vantage point. Look down to lushest vegetation. If green, dig a ditch at base of lush area—and hope it will fill with water. Vegetation on flat desert doesn't mean much, however.

(e) Dry stream beds offer best chance of water at lowest point of the outside of any bend. Terraces above dry riverbeds may yield water.

(f) Shale/sediment/clay areas are often productive if you dig— especially under bluffs. If moist.

(g) Sand dunes at seaside: Try at lowest point between dunes on outer edge. If you hit moisture don't dig too deeply, you might reach salt water—stop and let hole fill with fresh water. Dig a number of holes (some just above high-water mark).

(h) Dry desert islands often produce water in hole dug in hollow about 100 yards beyond and above high-tide mark. Don't dig too deep. About 12 inches enough following signs of seepage.

WATER PURIFYING

Treat all water as if polluted. Crystal-clear water could be contaminated. Tap water polluted. Mountain stream running from a high village or over a dead sheep.

Risks of cholera, typhoid, dysentery, or schistosomiasis too great— even though some survivors have drunk foulest fluids unpurified and gotten away with it.

Various methods to purify water—viz., when trapped in/exploring/ using-as-H-bomb-refuge an old lead mine, good water sources are pools. BUT surface of these invariably spoiled with skin of lead— equaling lead poisoning if drunk.

So . . . to purify: Place finger in ear, collect wax, dip finger in water for wax to break surface tension of lead layer, and drink from small area of now lead-free water (around where your finger was).

Basic steps for much more general use are:

(a) Strain all water through cloth or folded handkerchief to suspend grit/gravel/sand/rust/dust, and

(b) Boil hard for at least a minute (longer preferably) then let any sediment settle. Containers for boiling can be made from length of bamboo/paper box/inner-birch-bark pan (see *TOO EMPTY*), or

(c) Add five drops of iodine to 2 pints of water (or ten drops to cloudy water). Let stand for thirty minutes. Sterilize mouth of container with drop of water and wait a little longer.

(d) Pinch of salt can improve taste, or pouring water from can to can to can.

(e) Water-purifying tablets—for which follow instructions on bottle.

Note: Water seeping through sand into hole will be freshest on top, brackish underneath. Skim off top layer with large shell (also useful for digging). But brackish water won't kill you when sipped in small doses.

SURVIVAL STILL

Providing desert castaway has 6 foot square of plastic sheeting he can try to "milk" the ground. It does not work everywhere, but in many places could yield a pint a day or more.

Dig hole in unshaded spot 3 feet across, and deep enough to contain water bucket (or other wide-mouthed container) 2 inches below the lowest point of plastic sheet stretched over hole and weighted down in center with fist-sized rock. Taper the hole in towards bucket (as shown).

Anchor plastic with soil and rocks at rim of hole. Place rock in center to weight sheet down. (If you roughen undersurface of plastic with sand, it helps water dropets to drain more efficiently—but see it's clean). Note: Plastic or rubber tube from container to surface lets you sip water without taking up the sheet.

Sun raises heat of air and soil under plastic to furnace pitch. Forces vaporization of water present in ground soil. When air under plastic becomes saturated droplets form on plastic sheet, *it* being cooler than damp air below it. Drips trickle into container. Works at night as soil temperature is hot and plastic cool.

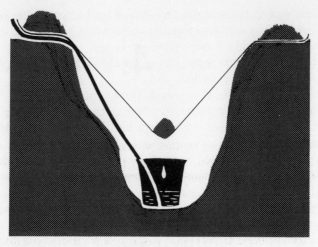

Survival still

Ensure plastic does not touch the earth anywhere and so lose moisture to the sand. Nor touch the bucket. Vapor mist underneath sheet will show when condensation is forming.

Patience is essential. You may get a pint in 24 hours, possibly a quart. Water is distilled and may taste flat. Add salt or pour from one can to another. Plastic catches rain, too, of course. And frogs, snakes and small animals may crawl in and be unable to escape—food.

N.B. Some sites yield more than others. One above bed of rock could soon run out of moisture. But a pint a day is possible even in a bad site. Good site might give quart a day for a month. As output decreases be ready to move still to new site. One still is not enough for survival in burning heat, but two or three would help to save you.

SOLAR STILLS

Secure these inflatable balls (which evaporate salt water to produce fresh water) to life rafts and float out on sea whenever sun is shining, so that you get as much drinking water as can be manufactured.

DESALTING KITS

If carried in your boat, use when you need water. Keep them stored if you have solar stills working in sunlight, or if it rains.

4: TOO WET

Swept up by flood, shaken by turf, windmilled by sluiceway—even a strong swimmer can drown. Swept out to sea/lake center/mid-estuary, the average swimmer may never return alive.

Out of his depth, the nonswimmer often goes out of his mind with fear. Sobbing/gagging/bubbling, he might take someone else with him (a panicking, drowning man finds astounding strength).

THERE IS NO SUBSTITUTE FOR LEARNING TO SWIM AND LIFESAVE UNDER PROPER INSTRUCTION. Even so, everyone can try to do something in water and—starting with a deep breath—possibly survive.

BEFORE SPLASH-DOWN
(IF YOU HAVE TIME)

Kick off waders/boots/shoes.
Rip off tight/heavy/woolen clothing.
Leave on shirt/trousers/blouse/dress/pajamas.
Stuff clothing and pockets with any buoyant objects.
Buoyancy equals balls, sponges, plastic bottles, bags, boxes, etc.
Remember buckets/bins/boots-upside-down float.
Take any "raft"—plank/car seat/spare wheel and tire.
Don't miss any handy life belt or life jacket.
Aim for anything floating on water.
(Taken-off clothing—e.g., raincoat—should be taken with you if a swimmer so you can improvise buoyancy with clothes. See later.)

IF YOU CANNOT SWIM

1. GASP IN AIR BEFORE SPLASH-DOWN.
2. GRIT TEETH TIGHT WHEN SINKING.
3. FIGHT OFF PANIC.
4. MAKE LIKE A BOTTLE NOT A BATTLE.
5. DON'T THRASH/SPLASH/STRUGGLE.

6. LET NATURAL BUOYANCY BRING YOU UP.

Blow out and breathe in when mouth breaks surface. Don't try to swim. *Nor raise arms*. You can attempt to float like a corked bottle in any of three ways—SO LONG AS YOU DON'T PANIC.

(a) Face up: Head back and out of water, body vertical. Hold breath as long as able. Press palms down just below surface when going for air, to make sure mouth is out of water. Breathe out and in in close succession—vigorously.

(b) Face down: back of head out of water, body tilted diagonally. Bring face up to breathe with kick of legs and hands pressed down. Breathe out and in in close succession. Duck face under and repeat.

(c) Knees up: spine showing above water, head underwater near knees. Hold knees to chest with both hands. Lift head to breathe out and in quickly.

YOU MUST NOT PANIC. This is the crux. And it is very likely the nonswimmer WILL panic unless he has some floating object to hang on to.

IF YOU CAN SWIM

Deal with hazards immediately:

CURRENT CARRYING YOU OUT TO SEA

Don't panic and flounder.

Try to attract attention—waving ripped-off trunks/bathing suit/clothing—and shouting (see *TOO LONELY*). Float, tread water or swim slowly.

Check if you are still in deep water on long sloping beach by treading water—then sinking. Worth trying in various places even when apparently long way out.

Work out which way current is taking you. If on the slant then swim *with* and across it to emerge further along the shore. Swim your favorite stroke, resting frequently whenever tired. Never battle current direct.

If on an air mattress . . . *stay aboard* in most noncapsizable position. If narrow enough try swimming with hands as you lie along center. Don't fight against current, but tack diagonally after calculating how far out and how fast you are being taken. And aim to beach mattress farther along coastline.

Never be lured into chasing beach balls/toy yachts/air mattresses floating out to sea: Better to lose a ball or toy than a life. But if snared into this situation—*use whatever buoyancy support object offers* for return swim to help save energy.

GETTING CRAMP

Don't panic. Float on back using minimum effort.

(a) In foot: Grasp toes and try to bend towards shin.

(b) In calf: Straighten leg; try to bend toes towards knee and force foot back towards shin—pressing heel away.

(c) In thigh: Bend knee and stretch thigh forward.

When cramp eases, knead with fingers until hardness gone.

Important: *Stretching* combats cramp. And cramp twinges give advance warning of seizure-to-come. When warned stretch muscles immediately.

IN WATER, FLOATING WITH ICE

Swim violently for anything that will lift you out: ladder/boat/solid ice. Bitterly cold water will knock breath out of you, subtract any grip you have with fingers, and "curl" you up with shock.

Life span is usually shorter than thirty minutes in icy water. And can be a good deal less.

If water is cold but not cold enough to "curl" you up with chill spasm, conserve energy by minimum exertion (unless a landing near-by) by not removing clothing/swimming far/struggling. Cling onto wreckage if possible.

WHIRLPOOLS/FALLING DEBRIS/SHIP'S PROPELLERS

Zoom away from danger with fast crawl/side stroke/breast stroke until free from crisis zone. But don't miss any buoyancy at hand (raft/wreckage/barrel) which could help save you—and which is towable.

BURNING OIL/ONCOMING BOAT/GUNFIRE

Tread water. You will have to deflate a life jacket first. Kick hard and bob out of water. Point toes. Press legs together. Straighten body. Sink below. When underwater sweep hands (palm outwards) from thighs to above head in outstretched motion. Double up and swim forward when deep enough.

Swim underwater slowly. Use breast stroke/dog paddle/breast stroke-with-flutter-kick.

But . . .

(a) Use exaggerated arm action with any of them.

(b) Following kick of feet, *glide* with arms to side before next arm movement.

(Note: Swimmers can dive headfirst in clear or definitely deep water without risk of injury from underwater obstacles. Do this by bending sharply from hips then using breast-stroke arm action to thrust deeper and leg kick *once feet are underwater*.)

In burning oil swim into the wind using breast stroke. Try to splash flames away from head and arms.

SPILLWAYS AND DAMS

Swim down for riverbed.

Water rushes over sill into foaming currents which circle around and backlash. Go for the top too soon and you may be bounced like a Ping-pong ball on a jet of water.

Swimming near a spillway

But at riverbed level current is released downstream. Follow this and surface farther down the river.

RAPIDS

If with canoe—hang on to it (see later).

Otherwise swim down any clear tongue of water (V-shaped with point arrowing downstream) in white water. Break into deep water at far end or into slack water behind rocks on way down.

Best way to track down deepest channel is from the top of a rock: Then you can look down on rapids around you.

Haystack waves at end of "V" tongue are usually caused by fast current hitting slow, deep water—barge through with hard, determined swimming.

TREE OVERHANGING FAST WATER

Avoid at all costs. Swim/row/paddle *hard* to evade.

If canoe or rowboat is turned broadside in willows, lean downstream so bottom of craft presents its rounded bottom to pile-up of current—and not its cockpit. Pull hand over hand along branches.

SURF

Don't be eager (especially at start or end of vacation) to get into water without first checking if SAFE. Many casualties where surf has been running. Can be fatal to go in isolated surf. Instead swim where marker system shows safe beach. Look for notices—ask local opinion.

Surf can be violent. Can turn angry in a matter of moments. It can KO/hammer/exhaust unversed swimmer who thought it shallow and harmless. Children often surf victims.

Never attempt to fight a battering from heavy surf or being dragged along by a racing current. Survival in big surf needs skill.

Basically, only chance for person who does go out in heavy surf (or who gets knocked in off a jetty or sandbank) is:
1. TRY TO SURF ON SUCH INCOMING WAVES AS POSSIBLE.
2. GRAB SAND WITH FISTS TO AVOID BACKWASH.
3. WHEN CLEAR OF WATER SCRAMBLE ABOVE HIGH-WATER MARK.

And if swept out by riptide (surf draining back to sea):
1. DON'T BATTLE AGAINST IT.
2. SWIM DIAGONALLY ACROSS IT.

After a distance varying from a few feet to hundreds of yards, swimmer is clear of riptide and should be able to regain shore (though perhaps mile or more down the coast).

Raise arm for distress signal. Keep calm. Float or tread water until help arrvies from lifeguard/strong swimmer with reel and belt/lifesaver (see later).

If no help near, fight down panic. Swim with breast or side stroke to save energy:

(a) Swim parallel to coast until you get back into the breakers rolling shoreward.

(b) Ride in on back of small wave. Just before it curls over and breaks—shallow dive through it.

(c) In big surf, swim shoreward in trough between waves. When big wave approaches get down to bottom and grab sand with fists to avoid being swept off feet by undertow. Push off bottom and swim on once it passes.

Surf lifesaving—see later.

LANDING ON ROCKS

Aim for where water hisses up rocks. Avoid where spray shoots up in explosions. Swim slowly in making approach. Save strength for grasping rocks.

Head for destination behind big wave in the breakers. Face shore and "sit" in water pulling feet up like buffers. If rebuffed on first attempt swim with arms, getting ready for next attempt. Repeat.

Seaweed can make water quieter in its lee. Don't swim over it as much as crawl, grasping the weeds to pull yourself along.

Swimming ashore from raft/dinghy/plane wear shoes and at least one layer of clothing. Life jacket is Number One survival aid when facing rocky landing.

TRAPPED BY SHEER SEA CLIFFS WITH NO LEDGES

When trapped and forced to swim for safety through rising tide— aim for rocks in the sea. Keep on layer of clothing *and shoes/boots/ sandals* (for landing).

Make a rope, if possible, from ripped-up towels/belts/shirts. But it must be long enough to reach from rock to rock. The ideal is a proper rope or line. Handle it as for climbing (see *TOO LOW*).

Strongest swimmer goes first, towing rope tied around his waist (with bowline knot). Person paying out rope should be *anchored to a rock* so that if a wave takes the swimmer he won't be torn away too—and can field the swimmer who is being swept away.

When first swimmer reaches a rock, he too anchors himself before taking in the rope for the next swimmer—around the small of his back, feet braced against projection.

FLOODED TUNNEL/CAVE/PASSAGE

When roof meets water—duck.
But only when:
(a) You are certain that waterlogged barrier is only brief and caused by lowering of roof into water. And that on other side there will be air space again.
(b) It is essential and only way of escape is to try to wade (or possibly swim) through.

Strongest swimmer goes first—and is prepared to turn back if no way through. Take deep breath. *Feel* way.

1. VENT ANY BUOYANT CLOTHING WHICH COULD FLOAT YOU TO ROOF AND JAM YOU THERE.
2. USE ROPE OF BELTS/TIES/CLOTHES TO KEEP CONTACT.

System of signaling with rope:
One pull: "I'm O.K."
Two pulls: "Take in rope."
Three pulls: "Pay out."
Four pulls: "I'm there."

SKIN DIVING

Don't go—without proper training (which includes survival in emergencies).

SWIMMING FOR SURVIVAL

Best energy-conserving strokes: breast/side/back strokes.

Do them in whatever sequence suits. Swim strongly, but never directly against tide/current/wind: progress diagonally across. Side stroke possibly best for choppy water (easier to breathe).

If swamped by waves, breathe deeply whenever face is clear. Don't shatter yourself with perpetual swimming. Never give up. Keep going. Keep cool and rest often: floating on back/floating face-down/treading water.

Float on back whenever possible.

Float face-down when water choppy (as earlier). Body will tilt diagonally, back of head is out of water, and by sculling with hands you raise head to breathe—out then in.

Tread water by letting it do most of work—just hold mouth and nose out. Unless you have other preference, use scissors kick and scull with hands on or near surface.

A life jacket helps prolong time afloat (if wearing Mae West inflated by two carbon-dioxide cartridges, fire only one at first as inflation from both cramps swimming movement).

It is possible to stay afloat for hours without life jacket—especially in salt water. And with air trapped in clothing . . .

CLOTHING INFLATION

Taken-off clothes can be ballooned with air so they support you in water in *many* different ways. Such make-do floats . . .

(a) Need filling.

(b) Need careful handling as, if dragged down too hard into water, they let out air faster through material.

(c) Need competent swimming ability and, ideally, practice to construct and inflate.

(Note: Nonswimmer anticipating ducking and at water's edge could attempt to inflate raincoat/nylon shirt/blouse in readiness, and in absence of anything more solid available for buoyancy.)

UNDRESSING

Get rid of heavy/tight/wide-meshed clothing.

If chance something might serve as float (raincoat, say), don't jettison it right away but keep it floating on surface by trapping air in folds.

Kick off footwear but note: Boots held upside down with arms are floats. Hat can be used similarly.

Ideal clothing for floats: shirts/blouses/dresses/nightgowns/pajamas of man-made fibers or linen or cotton. When soaked they hold air the longest.

Remember not to strip completely: It is a fallacy everything must come off. Clothing helps combat cold. Only take off items which offer best air traps.

Undo zippers/buttons/hooks. When disrobing take deep breath after loosening everything and . . .

(a) Take off unbuttoned shirt like a coat (not over the head where it can get wrapped around face).
(b) Rip shirt front which doesn't button all the way.
(c) Stretch shirt down past waist as alternative.
(d) Rip shirt front which is buttoned but whose buttons are slippery and hard to undo.
(e) Push down undone pants to knees and farther; take deep breath and dip head under as you peel them off, using flutter kick to free them.

INFLATING

Knot clothes so that in each garment there is only one air opening—i.e., knot both trouser legs of pants near cuff end and zip or button up flies or side vents.

Knotting can be done directly in clothing or tied with tie/belt/stockings/garters.

Inflation is done with fast movement through the air, opening in clothing finishes up underwater, clothes balloon into buoyant sausages, and you hold opening under surface, possibly twisting tight.

WAYS OF INFLATING CLOTHING FLOATING ON WATER . . .

(a) Open garment opening as if to catch butterfly and scoop through air—either from behind back overhead and down in front, or in sidewinder move from side to side. Hold opening with hands below surface.

Then fill up by . . .
(b) Blowing up into downward-facing garment opening (under the surface).
(c) Taking air below surface in cupped hand and letting bubble fly up into garment opening.
(d) Splashing with a hand into garment opening.
(e) Pressing mouth against wet float and trying to force air through.

USING FLOATS

There are *many* variations in ways you can use buoyant clothing. If swimming, blow clothing up during resting period, then carry through water tied around waist when swimming until you need another rest.

Examples:

SKIRT. Keep on, and float on back. Lift hem, pull towards you then flick through air as if to cover knees. Curl hem back underwater to hold in island of air.

DRESS. Slip off. Knot it to block off neck and armholes. Fill. Grip with hands or possibly between legs.

TROUSERS. Hold inflated like a slingshot, chin resting in "V" of sausaged legs, fist gripping waistband which is tied with belt down about stomach level.

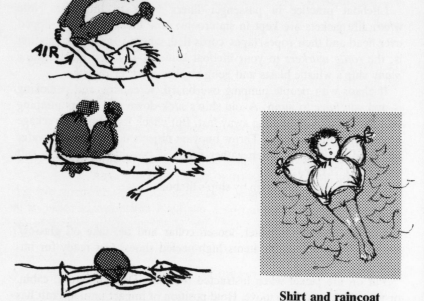

Trousers and skirt used as floats

Shirt and raincoat used as floats

Or slide arm through "V" of crotch and use same hand to secure waistband while swimming with other arm.

Or put chest through what now becomes "U" of crotch, and with each leg as a water wing swim breast stroke.

Or float on back and grip leg sausages between your own legs—meanwhile possibly inflating another garment.

SHIRT. Knot cuffs. Hold collar and shirttail and balloon into water to gather air. Quickly gather loose edges and you have bag and two sausages of air (sleeves).

RAINCOAT. Can be used (as shirt) to make big air sack.

SURVIVING WRECKS

Everything depends on not panicking. Even in fear-struck chaos, it is possible to keep your head (see *TOO CROWDED*).

SHIPWRECK

Carry out lifeboat drill. Assemble at proper station as directed by crew. Put on life jacket and help young/old/scared-stiff to put on theirs. Calm people down.

Lifeboat practice in passenger liners helps to this end. Note *where* life jackets are kept in stateroom; *how* life jackets are slipped over head and their ropes/tapes/cords tied; where *your* lifeboat station is; the *route markers* to your lifeboat station—say, red arrows; *how many* ship's whistle blasts and gong strokes warn of disaster.

If chaos with people jumping overboard, screaming and panicking —and you *have* to jump: Avoid ship's suck-down and others jumping on top of you by swimming away fast. But check for floating wreckage *before* and after jumping. Throw buoyant objects down first into water and land by it/them. Then gather more, if possible, to make a raft (see *TOO SLOW*).

Or you may be picked up by ship's lifeboat.

PLANE CRASH

Coming down over water, loosen collar and tie, take off glasses/ teeth/sharp or breakable items/high-heeled shoes. Get ready for impact (see *TOO FAST*).

Put on life jacket when instructed by crew. Don't inflate in cabin, or you won't be able to move. Hold position of impact until aircraft has stopped—there will be more than one terrific jolt.

(a) Release seat belt.

(b) Do as told by crew.

When outside, inflate life jacket. Cartridge-inflated life jacket for child should be inflated before fitting, otherwise noise can terrify.

Staff allocate dinghy places for all passengers and crew; take charge of dinghies; transmit radio distress signals; check dinghies all contain emergency rations and first-aid kits (see *TOO SLOW*).

CANOE CAPSIZAL

Stay with canoe. Much more buoyant and visible than you. Collect your paddle if you can.

Don't climb on/roll onto/*or try to right canoe*. Swim to one end. Tow or push to side and empty.

If danger from dam/rapids/rocks ahead, abandon it in good time and swim to side fast.

Warnings: Thundering sound/flying spray/silver line across river (showing edge of dam) . . . all indicate danger ahead.

If caught in rapids . . .

(a) Hang on to upstream end of canoe and swim down rapids, helping to swing it clear of rocks. Don't bother chasing paddle—someone else may get it for you.

(b) Swim to side *directly* heading at 90-degree angle for bank even though being swept downriver at same time.

SMALL-BOAT CAPSIZAL

Stay with it. You are much more visible with boat.

Cling/hang on/climb astride it. But leave it in good time if being swept to some worse fate: rocks/reefs/waterfall.

If you can right a dinghy/raft/boat, fair enough. But if not, simply keep with it and signal for help.

Flat-bottomed emergency rafts—if capsized—can be righted quickly with calm approach.

Squirm up onto bottom of raft, reach to far side, grasp lifeline (which goes round edge of raft) and skid back into water way you came —so flipping raft over. Often a handle is attached to center of raft bottom and you can use this.

If a righting line is floating from one side, toss it across bottom, move to the far side, and, holding it, bring feet up onto flotation tube and pull raft upright until it flips over.

Righting line can be improvised from belt/tie/rope.

Climb in on belly, squirming over thick end of one-man raft.

Have one man in water holding down one side of bigger raft, as rest clamber in over opposite side. But if on your own—climb in over end. Maneuver so wind is behind you when climbing in.

CAR UNDER WATER

Cars (and their passengers) crash into water from river banks/ roadsides/piersides/quarry tops.

(Note: Always park *alongside* water or, if no option, with brakes on and in reverse gear if facing. Seat belt being used heightens chances of survival *in* water.)

1. Car will stay afloat longer if window closed.
2. It is tremendously hard to escape with water pouring through windows. And door won't open because of outside pressure of water until car is nearly full.

However, if you can act before water is up to window level (which is rare due to impact/fright/surprise) and car is floating wheels down, wind down window and squirm through in nick of time.

Usual course is that car plunges under too quickly for this. Wait, and do as much of the following as your presence of mind allows.

1. WIND UP WINDOWS.
2. SWITCH ON ALL LIGHTS AT ONCE AS SOS SIGNAL.
3. DON'T TRY TO OPEN DOORS.
4. KEEP A HOLD ON DOOR HANDLE.
5. WAIT FOR WATER TO REACH CHIN.
6. THEN OPEN DOOR AND SWIM FOR TOP WITH DEEP BREATH.

While waiting for water to rise (which will be rapid), try to determine which way up you are. Hold children up into air pocket above water which will give you breathing space if door handles don't open at first.

Once water is to chin level, inwards rush of water from opening will be slight. If door sticks then try other doors/wind down window and squeeze out, pushing with feet. Kick or club through windshield or window if no other way.

Passengers should try to leave car together—if four doors. If not possible, make human chain—holding hands/clothes/hair so that door can't close and trap someone.

RIVER CROSSINGS

Hundreds of drownings happen each year all over the world when rivers have to be crossed by fording. Or whenever water has to be waded across. Always ask: Need this river be crossed? Isn't there some way around?

When it's "NO"—take survival action. Especially when emergency is forcing your hand.

WHEN TO CROSS

Will volume of river water get bigger or less? Very dangerous if in flood. And if a lot of debris is being carried down. Don't cross. Postpone it.

But if river is normal level and there are imminent signs of rains to come, get across fast (Note: Short, steep rivers rise and fall quickly, and flat, sluggish rivers take much longer.)

WHERE TO CROSS

Vital to study carefully. Most important safety factor of all. Time spent is rarely wasted. Look for . . .
(a) Clear banks. This gives you plenty of room to recover if you run into trouble.
(b) Firm, smooth riverbed without obstacles.
(c) Crossing free of logs, whirlpools, reefs, eddies, and other hazards particularly *downstream* of chosen place (which may appear excellent in itself).
(d) Current should be weak as possible. So choose widest part. Or place where river splits into several streams.
(e) Depth is important: Pick shallowest place. But you may have to swim.

HOW TO CROSS

Keep some clothes on to combat cold—so long as not baggy. Wear boots for grip and protection against boulders/sharp stones/holes. Carry rucksack (except when you may have to swim). This adds stability and balance through weight, and if packed well it can add buoyancy in a fall. But loosen straps for quick release if you stumble under.

Improvise on these basic methods.
(a) Straightforward wading with short shuffling steps. Move at right angles to bank. Face across stream. Hold on to boulders above or just under water. If current too strong, face downstream and move diagonally down and across to far bank but there *must* be room to move.
(b) Repeat as above but with a strong pole acting as a third leg. Place pole slightly ahead and upstream on riverbed then walk past it. And so on. Current keeps pole pressed down.

(c) If there are inexperienced or weak persons in your team, link arms in line. Weak person goes in middle.

(d) Ideally use a long pole as a rail, with *arms linked* and weakest person in middle. Strongest person is at upstream end. And you enter water to form a line up and downstream, not across the river. If weak person falls/stumbles/passes out, rest of team can support him.

Only use a rope when needed. If as a handrail, keep it high so you can grasp it while negotiating boulders. Don't use in wide/flooded/deep river where it can sag under surface.

If someone is trying to cross, he can tie bowline around waist and be paid out (see *TOO LOW*), but make sure you have room at side of banks—if he falls he will have to be paid out and brought in at right angles *not pulled back upstream* (and underwater).

Crossing river with exhausted person

LIFESAVING

Many lives are lost each year by brave people who try to save lives but who have no technique. Lifesaving in water means rapid judgment/sound knowledge/considerable skill/swimming ability.

In many circumstances it is better not to go to help of drowning person if would-be rescuer is not trained, since two lives might be lost.

Nonswimmer can sometimes help by throwing or holding a stick or some buoyant object which someone in water can grab.

It is possible for a strong swimmer, although not trained in lifesaving, to swim out with a stick or some object by which the drowning person can be towed (so long as he is able to hang on to it, *and is not brought into direct bodily contact with rescuer*).

FEAR is greatest enemy of people in difficulty, and endows them with abnormal strength: Something to be feared at all costs by rescuer. Strong swimmer (untrained in lifesaving) who decides to go to the rescue *must keep away from drowning person's reach* and tell victim he must grip the stick/pole/branch he is offering.

Ways by which nonlifesavers might help:

REACH

Casualty may be within reach from water's edge. Fling yourself flat and reach out with hand. Grip his wrist and have him grasp yours. Or if a little further out, hold pole/stick/plank/branch—anything for him to catch.

THROW

When farther out throw rope or any object that floats:
Beach ball/football/volleyball
Car seat
Spare car tire (will support eight people)
Planks
Poles
Fencing
Branch
Box
Wooden seat

Many things float. Cast around quickly for anything buoyant, and hurl. But don't go too far away—if drowning person thinks rescuer is deserting him, chances are he will panic and drown.

WADE

Wading out to drowning person where water is shallow is faster than swimming. Use pole you intend rescuing with to help wading (see river crossing).

ROW

Boat/canoe/punt will be fastest method to someone far from shore if craft available. Sight of approaching boat will also help drowning person to hang on longer and stay on top.

Important: On reaching the drowning person don't approach broadside, or side of craft will be clutched and you could capsize. Go in with bow or stern, instruct him to hang on and then tow to the side.

SWIMMING OUT-TO AND TOWING-BACK FOR INEXPERIENCED LIFESAVERS

Strip off most clothes unless a short distance (and then only abandon heavy or tight clothes). Speed is essential.

Jump in feet first (see *TOO HIGH*)—unless you know for certain the water is deep and clear and then you may prefer to dive. Conserve strength when swimming rather than race madly out to victim some way out.

Straight line as sea gull flies may not be quickest way at all. You may have to swim downstream in flowing river to try to cut off victim as he comes past. Or there may be a sandbar which shortens swimming distance. Remember—you must arrive with enough energy.

Take pole or object to offer the drowning person. A strong swimmer will know which strokes suit him best, but side stroke is strong and reliable for longish distances (simple and relatively small energy output). Arms can be changed. You can breathe in choppy water. And face is protected.

Or, if the swimmer prefers, swim on back—again using nontowing arm to assist in swimming.

BUT MAKE SURE YOU STAY OUT OF REACH WHEN YOU REACH THE VICTIM, AND AT ANY ATTEMPT TO GRAB YOU, KEEP OUT OF WAY OR BREAK THE GRIP SHARPLY. ONLY A TRAINED LIFESAVER SHOULD GO INTO RESCUE AT CLOSE QUARTERS.

If gripped (see *TOO CROWDED*).

MOTHER SAVING CHILD

Where child falls into water, and there is nothing to reach with or throw, or child is baby/toddler/infant . . .

(a) If mother cannot swim she should get in the water and hold on to land, lying flat out in the water and extending arms and legs to child.

(b) If mother can swim she should go to rescue, then hold child's head, one hand on either side of its face, and swim on back, supporting child on the forearms and chest, keeping the child's face out of the water.

SURF LIFESAVING

If YOU are on a beach bordering surf, you may be asked to handle the line and reel (attached to nonbuoyant belt worn by lifesavers) used by lifeguards.

If so, and with help from others if possible . . .

1. WATCH THE BELTMAN.
2. GET SIGNALS STRAIGHT.
3. NEVER PULL IN TOO FAST AND SO SUBMERGE RESCUER AND VICTIM.

FEELING CAPABLE AND BEING SO ARE VERY DIFFERENT. If not trained to lifesave, beltman must realize the MANY risks. He must be a strong swimmer/cool/know his limits.

If someone decides to go, recheck instructions. Make sure helpers on the line know the score too. If beltman then you . . .

4. PUT ON THE BELT.
5. SWIM OUT, DIVING UNDER BREAKING WAVES.
6. DON'T GRAB STRUGGLER BUT STAND OFF AND RE-ASSURE.
7. TELL CONSCIOUS VICTIM TO TURN BACK TO YOU.
8. GRIP FROM BEHIND HOLDING ONE OF VICTIM'S WRISTS TO HIS CHEST.
9. SIGNAL TO BE PULLED IN.

Start artificial respiration immediately, if necessary, once out of surf—see below.

ARTIFICIAL RESPIRATION

KISS OF LIFE

1. LAY INJURED ON BACK.

Kiss of Life

2. SECONDS COUNT—DON'T DELAY BY CLEARING MOUTH AND THROAT OF OBSTRUCTIONS UNLESS CAN BE DONE AT THE WIPE OF A FINGER (WRAPPED IN HANDKERCHIEF).
3. TILT HEAD WELL BACK AND PUSH JAW UP TO OPEN THROUGH AIR ROUTE (IN "SWORD SWALLOWING" POSITION)—VITAL.
4. SEAL NOSTRILS WITH YOUR CHEEK OR PINCH WITH FINGERS.
5. TAKE DEEP BREATH, OPEN YOUR MOUTH WIDE AND SEAL IT TIGHT AROUND VICTIM'S.
6. BLOW INTO HIS LUNGS. WATCH FOR CHEST TO RISE. THEN TAKE YOUR MOUTH AWAY.
7. WATCH CHEST FALL WHILE TAKING NEXT DEEP BREATH (AND LISTEN FOR RETURN RUSH OF AIR).

If this doesn't happen—push injured's head farther back and try again to get exchange of air needed.

8. REPEAT PROCESS. DO FIRST SIX INFLATIONS QUICKLY. THEN AT TEN A MINUTE FOR AN ADULT; TWENTY LIGHTER BREATHS A MINUTE FOR A CHILD.

Note: Often possible to clear injured's mouth after first 6 quick breaths. Quickly. Then carry on at rate specified above.

9. IF UNABLE TO OPEN OR USE INJURED'S MOUTH— USE MOUTH-TO-NOSE METHOD BY SEALING IN- JURED'S MOUTH AND BLOWING THROUGH HIS NOSE INSTEAD (USING SAME PROCEDURE AS MOUTH- TO-MOUTH).

If victim is injured about the face use . . .

SILVESTER METHOD (REVISED)

Act fast:
1. LAY PATIENT ON BACK.
2. PAD UNDER SHOULDERS WITH COAT/SWEATER/LIFE JACKET.
3. CLEAR MOUTH QUICKLY OF DEBRIS. BE SURE HEAD IS HANGING BACK AND DOWN.
4. KNEEL ASTRIDE HEAD, GRIPPING WRISTS.
5. CROSS THEM OVER LOWER PART OF CHEST.
6. KEEP YOUR ARMS STRAIGHT AND ROCK DOWN ON CHEST.

Silvester method of resuscitation

7. SWING BACK AND SWEEP INJURED'S ARMS UP AND OUT TO FULL SPAN (which takes pressure off chest and invites intake of air into patient's lungs).

8. REPEAT ABOUT 12 TIMES A MINUTE.

HAZARDS

Drowning is the hazard; artificial respiration the answer. Also vital for electric-shock/gas-fumes/choking/suffocation and other victims whose breathing has stopped.

Get injured to fresh air. And make sure any electrical contact is broken.

5: TOO BRIGHT

Dazzle is a fireball to the eyeball whether from bomb, zooming headlights, throbbing sun, forked lightning, flaming gasoline, glaring snow or electric arc.

Flash comes under/over/sideways—*through*. It is a red curtain. Yellow stars. Pink pain. Orange ball. Thick green light. Black band. Gritty tears. Unless you can help your eyes filter a paroxysm of light you may be blinded (see *TOO DARK*).

As subtle as a blackjack, glare often advertises its coming—from banner headline proclaiming nuclear war to storm clouds heralding lightning; from repeated car-lights dazzle to persistent sun-flash from snow. Be ready.

STOPPING GLARE

HUGE FLASH

This usually signals a kicking explosion either to come almost simultaneously or to follow.

Throw yourself flat on the ground. Hurl children/old people/companions with you. If shade immediately available dive and roll into it —under window/in ditch/behind tree. Shout that others stay on ground.

Blink reflex will help you: Eyes screw shut/head jerks away/hands mask eyes. Keep eyes shut tight. Prepare for potentially tremendous BANG by grasping base of skull with interlocked fingers. Wrists squeezing ears.

Dig elbows into floor. Keep eyes closed. Lock fingers together hard. Force head down. Count to 100 slowly before opening eyes behind fingers of one hand made into slits (H-bomb flash lasts twenty seconds and could fade before blast comes, up to sixty seconds longer)—keep other hand pressing on neck.

If driving car reflex actions will be to stab brakes/close eyes/fling hand to face. If after flash-shock you have not crashed and are still in one piece, keep head down, eyes slitted and make for side as non-skiddingly as possible. Duck below windows and wait for BANG.

Blindness from gigantic glare may not be permanent: From several seconds to days of darkness is an estimate, but could last longer if flash happens in the dark.

STRONG GLARE

Screen eyes as shown to combat sunlight reflecting from snow/water/sand. Use these protective measures even when sky is overcast as harmful rays can still penetrate and hurt your eyes.

People differ in reaction to strong glare. Even though you may not seem troubled, always wear eye protection in areas of brightness. Penalties for not doing: You will be unable to see far; judgment may falter; night vision could be affected.

Following methods of making eye shades have proved effective— try to use (a) and (b) in conjunction with any one of the others for maximum safety.

(a) Peer from under pulled-down cap peak/hat brim/helmet rim/eye shade.

Eye shades

(b) Rub shoe polish/mud/grease/burnt cork/anything blackening on upper cheeks and around eyes to cut down sun-ray reflections.

(c) Make goggles from paper/cardboard/camera film/leather/wood/ plastic by cutting slits (either——'s or +'s) in material to peer through. Tie around head with string or laces, tape or bit of elastic from underpants.

(d) Hair, leaves, grass, reeds or moss can be held over eyes by clamping to brow with broad "tape" tied around head.

(e) A face mask of thin material (say handkerchief) has saved eyes.

(f) Dark or smoked glasses have disadvantages—they let light in at sides and from below; they can break; they mist (smear with soap) or frost up.

Tie down any eye shade which flaps—like handkerchief over face —with tape/string/cord. This will stop sun rays reflecting UP from snow/water/sand—most acute light bounce of all.

Keep using eye protection once your eyes have suffered from sun-blindness and recovered. They will be sensitive to normal bright light as well as glare, and should be screened even on dull days.

Remember, too, ultraviolet rays will attack the *skin* in bright light (before you have chance to become suntanned), if you are suddenly pitched into an area of glare. Shield body instead of stripping off by:

(a) Buttoning down sleeves and wearing pants over all of legs.

(b) Turning up shirt collar and buttoning up neck.

(c) Making headgear as near to that of Arabs as possible.

Expose body to sun for five minutes a day until you become tanned. Even then only bare skin to sun for short periods each day.

Arab headgear

INTERMITTENT DAZZLE

Possible sources: headlights/mirror/flashlight. Sudden dazzle from any of these could hypnotize and draw you toward them in moment of glare.

Look beyond and to one side. Drivers look to the right, for example.

WHEN WARNED OF GLARE

THE BOMB

(See also *TOO HOT/TOO FULL*.)

WARNING: Radio/TV/newspaper reports of mounting tension; official U.S. Civil Defense warning system is siren-sound for five to seven minutes. Public takes shelter and receives further instructions through Emergency Radio Broadcasting System. (See *TOO FULL*.)

FLASH is first onslaught of exploded nuclear bomb (followed by *blast* then *radiation*—see *TOO FULL*). Coupled simultaneously with heat (see *TOO HOT* for fire fighting), the *flash-heat wave* throbs from a miniature sun to assault those outside this fireball's immediate devastation area.

Sudden huge flash action already treated.

If warned of fantastic light-heat spasm ahead by rising/falling sirens . . . rush home unless more than five minutes away. Otherwise find shelter. Give anyone shelter if you are already indoors and stay there. If outside seek shelter in any shade offered. Priorities are:

1. Any solid-object cover.
2. Ditch/trench/gutter.
3. Furrow/dip/fold.
4. Flat on ground.

Cover exposed skin on hands/head/neck with anything available. If nothing, use coat as head-and-hands hood, and pin down with elbows as you lie. If no flash after several minutes and better cover available, dash to that.

If sirens rise and fall as you are driving, pull off road or along curb—if possible—away from any bottleneck or obstacle that could obstruct fire engine/civil defense vehicles. Jump out and hurl body into available cover.

INDOORS: Use anything solid as flash-fire shield; run under strong table/down into cellar/under staircase; crouch below or between windows on flash side if room bare. Stay until blast past.

IF NEWS IS BAD, ADVANCE PREPARATION AGAINST NUCLEAR ATTACK: Follow advice given at time in newspapers/over radio/on TV. At time of writing, these precautions help if you are given some time (see *TOO FULL* for advance preparations against blast and fallout. Also *TOO HOT*):

(a) Check under roof for chinks which could let in flash rays—which are also heat rays. Stop them up with nonflammable material.

(b) Clear away any potential source of fire under roofs/in attics/by ventilators/near windows: piles of papers, magazines, letters, old rubbish.

(c) Whitewash all windows thoroughly, especially at top of house, to bounce back flash-heat waves. And to reflect rather than absorb light (later blast will shatter glass but you may have stopped flash blindness/fires/scorching).

(d) Have fire-fighting aids ready (see *TOO HOT*).

(e) Fireproof all burnable material in house (see *TOO HOT*). Consider staying elsewhere if house is bungalow/single-story prefabricated house/house trailer/or top-floor apartment. (Best floors in multistory offices are middle ones, unless block only four stories or less high when ground floor probably best.)

LIGHTNING

WARNING: obvious storm signs; hair crackling/standing on end/sparking; metal on ice axes/spades/scissors/guns/golf clubs singing.

Lightning is one of the most unpredictable forces in the universe. It can frizzle you to nothing in a field or club down a house and leave you unharmed. Perhaps 20 miles long, a flash of lightning can strike repeatedly in same place (e.g., Empire State Building struck several times each year).

Around 20 million thunderstorms strike the earth each year. Chances of being hit?—about 2.75 million to one. These points may help you heighten the odds.

INDOORS: Unplug TV. Put away knives and scissors. Never stand in front of windows. Close all windows (glass is bad conductor of lightning). Sit toward middle of room—virtually 100 per cent safe. Car (without a flat) is one of the safest places to be.

OUTDOORS: Keep away from skyline/vertical faces/underground openings (say caves where ionization of air could attract lightning flash). Don't go blithely into rock-face cracks/caves/fissures as lightning could still get through. Any wet surface (cracks in rocks) heightens the risk. Don't get under rock/snow/earth overhangs as lightning can spark from lip of overhang to the ground and fry you in the gap of a ready-made spark plug. Jettison anything metal.

Avoid tree shelter if possible—especially oak, elm, poplar. Steer clear of structures like steel bridges/brick-built bridges/tall chimneys.

Old barns fairly safe for shelter. But out in center of open field best. Or any flat ground rather than steeply angled—even small ledge/terrace/etc. Squat on balls of feet if rubber soles, head down. Don't double contact and destroy insulation by steadying yourself with hand on wall/floor/cave side. Never be at highest point of landscape.

DRIVING

WARNING—Whenever you take a walk/car/bike on roads at night, in daytime fog or snow, remember that dazzle from headlights IS dangerous. It takes eyes about four seconds longer to recover from strong glare. At 40 mph a car will travel the length of nearly 40 coffins during this time of blind driving. Reduce speed when dazzled. If really blinded, stop.

Don't declare war on the roads. Amount you are dazzled depends partly on amount you dazzle others with *your* lights.

Don't provoke retaliation from cars/trucks/busses (possibly with *much greater lighting power* than your vehicle) by:

(a) Retaliating with full beam against cars you *think* not dimmed.

(b) Driving behind cars with headlights "up," and so perhaps provoking a feud.

(c) Driving with headlights on full beam continually.

(d) Having your headlights misaligned so they dazzle others without your realizing it.

(Note: Check handbook for manufacturer's instructions on angles of dip and sideways deflection of headlights to see if they differ and follow accordingly.

If adjustment is needed, car manual gives directions. Or go to a garage which has right equipment.

Or, if possible, have lights checked at a service station.)

FLASH HAZARDS

BLINDNESS

Atomic-flash-caused blindness is usually only temporary—as is sunblindness (see *TOO DARK*).

FLASH BURNS

High-voltage electricity jumping can blacken skin to alarming degree. Cleaned off, much of skin could well be found intact and nowhere as bad as feared (see *TOO HOT*).

LIGHTNING FLASH

Can shred off clothing with bizzare effects/scorch/break bones/lacerate/stop breathing—depending where person is and what holding (e.g., gun/gardening fork/ice axe). Treat accordingly (shock, lacerations and fractures—*TOO FAST*; burns— *TOO HOT*; stoppage of breath—*TOO WET*).

Lightning protection

SUNBURN

Ultraviolet rays redden, burn and blister skin before it tans. Can cause pain/fainting/shock. Limit skin exposure to sun in dazzling brightness to five minutes a day. Then cover as described earlier. Also prevent with sunburn ointment. Coconut oil helps.

Treat with shade/rest/coolness. Lots to drink. Fan. Don't smooth on greasy ointments. Don't re-expose until completely healed. No stimulants.

MIRAGE

Water/snow/sand can shimmer with frequent images: lapping wavelets on hot sand; cities in sky; marching soldier from shrubs; fleet of sailing ships from birds on water. Don't let mirages rob your judgment or balance.

View from different heights and angles to see them change shape and/or vanish.

6: TOO DARK

What do you do when the light goes out? How do you grope, paw, feel, claw, fumble and stumble out from the darkness? How do you fight paralyzing fear?

Blinded by snow glare/bomb flash/acid splash, blinkered by pepper/fumes/smoke, shuttered by shattered bulbs/dirty windshield/power cut, or blacked out by the night. . . there is little more overwhelmingly terrifying.

More so when other predicaments crowd around: freezing cold, fast car, strange room, open sea, mysterious forest, burning bingo hall, groaning ice.

WHEN THE LIGHT GOES OUT

GET SAFE

Stay where you are if secure. If not crawl/grope/feel to nearest safest point using memory, if possible, to avoid rubble collapse, live wires, deep water, spilled chemicals, weakened flooring or other hazards not possible to check safely once you are in the dark.

If driving, stop as nonskiddingly as possible. Reflexes should automatically steer you away from any head-on collision—except you may then collide with road-edge hazard. Don't jam on brakes when road is open (eye can retain image of what's ahead for about a twentieth of a second). Brace for crash (see *TOO FAST*) if at all possible.

TAKE STOCK

Check pockets/handbag/immediate surroundings for sources of light. Memorize. Listen. Smell. Only move if you have to—if forced to shift through fire or flood. If chances of rescue good or of light returning, stay and make yourself comfortable. If no immediate chance of aid plan action to help yourself. Try to evaluate best way to signal for help. Think out best escape route: emergency exit/porthole/window or fissure in the rock.

KEEP TOGETHER

Don't stray apart. Stay within touching distance of next person. If one person has to go ahead keep contact with him by a rope made from anything handy—belt/ties/towels.

KEEP YOUR NERVE

(See also *TOO LONELY*.)
Don't get rattled—tremendously easy thing to do. Be ready for anything to unnerve you. Phosphorescent objects (like logs in jungle). Spiders' eyes glow in beam of flashlight. Dripping water. Bats flying. Wind moan. Shadows. Water gurgle (lapping cave water can sound like voices). Owl/cat/bird cries. Animal screams. Rustle of grass. Cistern filling. Arctic emptiness.

Noise is psychologically more unnerving than the dark itself. In long periods of darkness combat eeriness by talking/shouting/playing radio/praying.

MOVING IN THE DARK

Use senses in a rough order of priority: (1) sight where possible, (2) touch, (3) memory, (4) sound, (5) smell. Circumstances could change this order: Sight might be useless in thick smoke and touch would take over. Sometimes sound can be the initial radar—by throwing sticks/stones/coins to determine dangerous areas ahead.

1: SIGHT

Light fire (see *TOO COLD*). Scrape sparks with shoe nails. Use camera flashbulbs and their gun. Employ any battery-powered light (slide viewer/toy spaceship/flashing robot). ANY source of light is morale-boosting—even a luminous watch face.

Use as little light as necessary. E.g., only moon and starlight if walking on terrain known to be safe. Flashlight uses up batteries, bulbs and "blinds" your night vision. Get eyes used to dark, pupils wide-open scavenging for any stray light rays. Other senses too will get more acute. Ration lighting as morale-charger and energy-booster.

Save light *when* using it. Don't chain-light precious matches/lighter/ flashlight by continually striking, flicking or keeping batteries switched on. Instead conserve at all costs by . . .
(a) Using paper mini-spills to eke out matches. Make from 2-inch

wide strips of paper which, with a little practice can be rolled as tight as stiff wire. Start by wetting thumb and forefinger of left hand and rub back and forwards at one corner of paper strip. Suddenly it will roll diagonally and *very* tightly when done properly. Light spill as match flame is about to die.

(b) Burn match/lighter/flashlight in short spells and use image-retaining powers of eye. (1) Light match, (2) look around, (3) travel several yards as soon as light goes out. You improve with practice.

(c) Flashlight battery lasts longer in short bursts. Keep batteries next to your body when not using, as warmth restores even a spent battery.

(d) Watch with luminous dial sometimes gives enough light to read small print (telephone number/address on envelope/words when jotting message). Can also be used as a marker for any strategic point in dark room—by fireplace/ventilator/window.

Never trust eyesight wholeheartedly in limited light. There is danger of all manner of deception: the 400-foot cliff which from above looks like a 10-foot step; the deep pit underground which resembles a puddle; the outer door of train which reflects toilet door.

2: TOUCH

Use hands as antennae. Arms should sweep as wide an area as possible. Raise hands in front to feel for obstructions. Don't touch with fingers—and risk gripping live wires. Instead . . .

(a) Use back of hand, or

(b) Clench fist extending one knuckle. Circle fist when probing so any live wire would probably graze knuckle first. And save you.

Go on hands and knees only as last resort. Prefer feeling around walls of wherever you are standing up. Faster, safer, more energy-saving. Go low to cooler, clearer air in smoke or fumes, however. Or if floor very uneven.

Keep in touch with everyone else. Hold hands, waists or heels (if crawling). Keep hand on wall.

Use pole/billiard cue/branch as feeler to jab ahead in pitch blackness. But extra care is need if chance of live wires anywhere around.

Don't rush from place to place in darkened room. Feel around the walls until you find a door or window. Move methodically. Remember your watch can be a luminous marker for any strategic spot.

3: MEMORY

Don't trust it, but there are times when it is useful. Moving from landmark to landmark, each approximately remembered, is main memory application. Remember . . . bearings you know like the back of your hand go haywire in darkness/mist/smoke. And it is almost impossible not to overestimate distance in the dark.

4: SOUND

Noise is deceptive as well as helpful. Ears not as selective as are the eyes. Approaching car/train/rockfall could be followed almost simultaneously by another (either following or coming in opposite direction)—but noise sounds as all one. The noisier a place the harder to move when using sound as an aid. The ear has little discrimination.

Some sounds are invaluable. Surf/rapids/dams thunder a warning. Continual bird cries indicate possible roosting place on land.

Keep quiet yourself when moving in darkness. Don't shout, yell or bawl to fortify spirits (which it *does* do) when moving, but make least noise possible so you can listen for any guide or warning noise. Or cries of help from anyone else.

Use echoes to help you—they can give general indication of surroundings. For instance . . .

(a) Don't ignore the "sixth sense" of the blind which many claim is sound-bounce from nearby objects or empty spaces. (Note that this cannot be used below the waist—you cannot sense steps/pits/gaps in the ground.)

(b) Check any sixth sense you "feel" by chucking stones/coins/debris in the necessary direction. Forget about trying to estimate depth of any hole by counting seconds until your missile hits the bottom. You will know if it's more than a few feet deep.

When an escape route is found—say door of smoke-filled room—wait by it if other people not at hand and repeatedly call and whistle so they are guided out to you.

5: SMELL

Only a very general guide. Hazards identifiable by odor—scorching/gas/sewerage. Some smells—like burning—carry for miles. Musty odor of mud flat/mangrove swamps/rotting vegetation or ozone can guide you to some extent.

ASPECTS OF DARKNESS

SEARCHING ROOMS

Search dark or smoke-ruined room with a definite plan if anyone could be trapped inside. Make complete circuit round the walls from the door, feeling especially in/under/on beds, tables, cupboards where people might have sheltered/flaked out/be trapped. Finally cross to room center diagonally from the door to check no one is lying there. But take great care in burning building as center of floor is weakest point and may collapse.

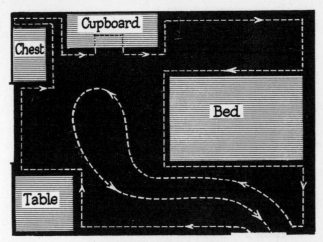

Searching dark room

HANDLING FIREWORKS/ROCKETS/SIGNAL FLARES

Use available light to read instructions—vital. Don't crouch over when lighting but keep at arm's length. Keep face clear. Much better to carry pyrotechnics in box than in pockets—and take out one at a time.

ON WATER

If you don't *have* to land on a strange coast from raft/dinghy/boat in the dark—don't. Wait until morning.

Out on the sea land can be reflected by clouds; dark-gray shades could mean open sea or land underneath; whiteness might mean ice and snow underneath. Listen for cries of birds coming from one direction—possibly roosting place on sea edge. Listen for far-off sounds of water pounding on rocks/reefs/ beach.

ON MOUNTAINS

Wait until morning on unknown or dangerous terrain. Take shelter (see *TOO COLD*). Don't try to follow water downhill—very risky fallacy: Think—*this entails waterfalls*. Never judge ground by shadows. Avoid having to climb down rock steps in darkness—it is impossible to gauge their real height.

ON SNOW

Overcast sky can mean a drastic lack of contrast on snow-plastered ground. It becomes impossible to judge nature of terrain at all. Don't move about in a whiteout. You could walk over cliffs, into crevasses, through cornices. It can be hard to stand up straight. No horizon/depth/dimension. Discarded soup cans might look like steel oil drums, and vice versa.

Wait as calmly as possible until settings resume shape and structure (see *TOO COLD*).

IN JUNGLE/FOREST/WOOD

Any woodland seems extensive at night. Extensive woodland is frightening. Foliage canopy clamps down blackness. Creepers/vines/branches look like snakes. Creaks and groans add to movement of trees. Animal and bird noises are magnified. Light fire if possible (contain it against any forest-fire risk). Building a fence around your camp may help to give feeling of security.

IN CAVE/MINE/SEWER

Keep up morale from the start. Be ready for water echo: dripping/booming/gurgling. Subterranean sounds can become oppressive. Keep together. Pause on threshold of darkness to let eyes become accustomed to gloom. Don't shout when moving—though it can be a good vent to feelings when resting.

Rest flashlights and lights frequently. Keep looking back. Many ways to signpost your route—cardboard arrows pointing back, drips of candle wax on floor, length of string, thread or rope. Avoid (in scenic limestone caves) blazing a trail of soot marks, smashing stalactite formations, or scratching on rock—use if possible a method that doesn't desecrate beauty.

Never rush when wading along underground waterways and be prepared to swim if floor suddenly disappears. Shallow pools could turn out to be deep.

DIRECTION IN THE DARK

Stars always give direction.

NORTHERN HEMISPHERE: The North Star is always within one degree of true north. Locate the Big Dipper (or Great Bear) which appears like a large saucepan with the two stars on the side farthest from the handle pointing to the bright Polaris or North Star.

Big Dipper and North Star

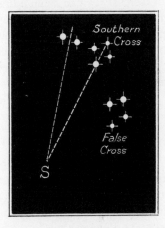

Southern Cross

SOUTHERN HEMISPHERE: North Star is invisible, but the Southern Cross indicates south. Find its four bright stars in a closely knit cross (don't pick the false cross to its right and with dimmer stars set farther apart), and spot the two bright stars set together on its left. A line bisecting these two at right angles points directly south. Also, the line straight down the Southern Cross points south—approximately. Where the two lines intersect is exact south (in a very starless sector of sky known as the Coal Sack).

When steering a course by sun (see *TOO SLOW*) and clouds obscure it, you can sometimes still find the sun. Hold knife blade/nail file/plastic credit card vertically on thumbnail (or anything glossy), and slowly rotate. Unless day is very dark, sun can cast faint shadow. Midday gives poor results. So does standing under trees.

DARKNESS ON THE ROADS

Many more accidents happen at night than in daylight. Road disasters pile up and up in fog/snow/rain.

Hazards double up when *TOO DARK*. When dark *and* wet expect the worst. Gloom plays such a factor in accidents it has been reckoned pedestrians are twice as safe during a full moon.

Danger times: around 5:00 P.M. each week-day. And after closing time each night, especially about 11:00 P.M. on Saturday evenings.

WALKING

If no pavement walk on left-hand side of road. Wear white— down to a handkerchief worn around neck or tucked into belt. Shine flashlight when traffic approaching—from either side.

Crisis point . . . on open road when sandwiched in lights of approaching vehicle and one coming from behind. Scramble up onto shoulder and keep on side until they pass. Remember—vehicle speed is an illusion at night; you can never be sure.

When crossing in built-up areas: Use crossings and islands (or underpasses or overbridges); don't step onto crossing until vehicles have *stopped* (see figure of girl jumping onto hood in *TOO LOW*); LISTEN and don't dive out.

DRIVING

Check *you* have no blind spots. Try this quick test.

Press back against a wall, arms outstretched like wings. Stare straight ahead. Stick your thumbs up. And move both fists forward levelly for about 6 inches. But keep looking ahead. Are you conscious of both thumbs? Especially the left one? If not make allowances when pulling out into (or back into) traffic stream. If blind spot is very accentuated it would be a grand idea to see an eye specialist.

Wide frames on spectacles might cause blind spots. Also—clean your glasses thoroughly in any dark driving conditions.

Ensure *car* has no blind spots: Clean windows.

Wipe all lights, reflectors and windows frequently—especially the windshield (both sides to clear off cigarette smoke and diesel-fume fallout). Damp cloth best, but wadded-up newspaper makes do.

Back of a comb will clean off ice/frost/snow.

Clean windshield wipers at same time. Keep windshield washer water unfrozen by adding alcohol or a little washing powder (to lower freezing point of water). If wiper motor fails in bad weather, disconnect wipers from motor, tie to a long loop of string thread in through both small side windows, and employ passenger working this endless belt (and wipers) until you reach a garage. Rub windshield with cut potato when wipers broken or missing. Or half an onion.

If windshield is hit by a flying stone and cracks into a milky blindfold—PUNCH IT! (straight over the steering wheel).

If a rear-light glass is smashed in dark/fog/snow smear lipstick over bulb to keep it red/legal/safe.

When crisis demands tricky reversing and no reversing light, use rear flashers to see by on crucial side.

In emergency (puncture/accident/wheel in ditch) reflect light back from headlights to crucial spot with wiped-clean hubcap.

There are three very vulnerable positions when conditions are *TOO DARK*:

(a) Instances like big farm trucks reversing into a field in dusk or fog with rear lights concealed in the gateway, and whole vehicle presenting a wall of steel across country road.

Remedy: Post a lookout at worst bend or blind hill nearby to wave down oncoming traffic. In any case . . . switch on full headlights and blow horn.

(b) Any vehicle making a left-hand turn off main road in thick fog.

Remedy: Flash headlights as well as directionals, and blow horn when making maneuver . . . but listen first with engine off for approaching traffic.

(c) Car driver who loses bearings in thick smog and veers out onto wrong side of road completely lost.

Remedy: Switch all lights on. Blow horn. Ease back right with flashers working.

DRIVING IN FOG: Hunch over steering wheel (you won't be going fast enough to be thrown through it if you have to stop quickly). Always use *dimmed* headlights whether day or night. Side lights alone are useless on their own. And full beam headlights throw a dazzling whiteout ahead.

Stick to busy roads. Keep behind a big truck—but at a distance (so his taillights are just visible). Truck driver will have best view of road ahead. His vehicle's bulk will stir up fog.

Don't try to overtake him in a clear patch: There is a grave danger that you will run smack into wall of fog while passing—cause of many pile-ups.

Curb yourself. Notice any landmarks on route to give you bearings. Keep wiping, cleaning, washing the windshield—and keep your glasses cleaned.

DRIVING AT NIGHT: If coming out of brightly lit building shut eyes as you take the driver's seat and let eyes adjust to darkness.

Don't exceed 50 mph with headlights on full beam even on clear, fine night with no oncoming headlights (ideal conditions); nor go over 38 mph with dimmed headlights in these perfect settings. These are the maximum safe speeds on ordinary roads (not freeways). Even less than half these speeds could still be unsafe when there is headlight glare from opposite direction, rain and fog patches. Reduce speed drastically in poor conditions. Don't drive more than two hours at a stretch.

Stay awake on long night drive by: changing seat position; having companion chat (but don't pick up hitchhiker: see *TOO CROWDED*); playing radio; stopping in turn-off and sleeping or taking short walk; pulling in at cafe or turnpike service plazas. Lick hand. Wet eyes with it. Stick head out of window.

Signs of falling asleep at car wheel (cause of many turnpike deaths) are:

Muscle spasms.

Jerking reflexes.

Straightening legs.

Suddenly talking in louder voice.

Yanking at steering wheel.

Stabbing at brake pedal.

Nodding.

Yawning.

Blinking.

Increased bursts of speed for no reason.

Nervous tapping on steering column/wheel/dashboard.

Driver on own *must* be ready for these signs. Passenger with driver displaying these signs should make him stop. But what if in middle of a freeway stretch? Pull in, get out, lift hood.

How can you wake up enough to get to a safe parking spot? Roll head around three times slowly in each direction. Take several deep breaths. Exhale in short bursts through clenched teeth and tightly drawn lips. It works for a short period. But stop to do it.

WHEN EYESIGHT FAILS

SUNBLINDNESS

Caused by sun flashing off snow/water/sand or just direct. And through your not wearing eye protection (see *TOO BRIGHT*). Eyes hurt, water, see red and black, burn, swell, discharge and feel full of grit.

Treat with wet cloth to soothe (but only if temperature is above freezing). Keep changing compresses when warm. Don't use eye drops or ointment. Cure is time. Eighteen hours may be sufficient. But then eyes become as sensitive as a fast camera film—keep them shaded/screened/*protected*.

FLASH BLINDNESS

Flash dazzle is usually fairly short-lived. If not possible to get to hospital, cover eyes with clean dry dressing—any clean cloth and hope for the best. Both eyes usually affected by a huge flash so, if only *one* eye cannot see, it could be something in the eye from flying fragments.

SOMETHING IN THE EYE

DON'T RUB. Blink instead. Many many times. If on own, try to see with a mirror. If not too painful could be under lower lid. If not visible here pull upper lid down over lower, hold for tears to wash. Blow nose vigorously closing nostril on opposite side. Wet twisted corner of a handkerchief to get the particle.

HELPING SOMEONE ELSE: Tell them to look up and pull lower lid gently downwards. Then tell to look down and draw upper lid up. Never move an object embedded in center of eye, but only when on eyelid or on "white" of the eye. Clean with clean water.

If object too tricky to remove, cover with clean dressing and get to medical aid as soon as possible.

BLINDNESS AFTER ACID/PEPPER/CHEMICAL SPLASH

Act fast . . . sluice eyes with any available water that is clean: tap/fire bucket/stream. Dip head under and rinse out eyes—holding them open and blinking at intervals. Flush for several minutes. Protect an unaffected eye with any handy cloth while doing this. Speed is crucial.

GUIDING THE BLIND

Don't despair by any means if someone is blinded (whether temporarily or permanently) and you have to get them to safety too. The following points may help:

1. NEVER MANHANDLE OR PROPEL A BLIND PERSON UNLESS VITAL. LET THEM TAKE YOUR ARM OR PLACE A HAND ON YOUR RUCKSACK/ELBOW/ ANKLE (IF CRAWLING).
2. ALWAYS SPELL OUT MOVEMENT DIRECTIONS IN EVERY DETAIL. LEAVE NOTHING OUT. THOUGH YOU MAY THINK IT HARDLY WORTH MENTIONING —IT IS.
3. ALWAYS ADDRESS A BLIND PERSON BY NAME.
4. SUCCESS WILL DEPEND ON YOUR TONE OF REAS- SURANCE AND COMPETENCE.
5. DON'T STARTLE BY YOUR SUDDEN PRESENCE WHEN BLIND PERSON THINKS HE IS ON HIS OWN.
6. AVOID CHANGING LAYOUT OF CAMP/ROOM/CAVE WITHOUT FIRST TELLING BLIND PERSON EVERY DETAIL OF THE CHANGE.

Blinded people have rock climbed/spelunked/canoed. They have cycled and skiied in tough conditions. Remember this when faced with guiding the sightless in survival settings.

Don't forget the blind dread movement. Especially the newly-blind —the kind you are very likely to be helping. Give every help and don't neglect. Keep shutting your own eyes to "feel" their predicament.

If *you* become blinded (by temporary flash blindness, say) in known surroundings and you *have* to move . . . use a long stick as a probe when on your own. Rather than shuffling head down and crouched, try walking erect, timing each step with the touch ahead of the stick. Tip explores zone where foot will go before it gets there, right foot steps forward onto it, meanwhile cane switches to where left foot will go. If stick reports sudden step/drop/obstacle, your body—with practice—stops upright in balance.

Keep trying this. And place ball of foot first rather than the heel.

7: TOO COLD

Cold that kills is not confined to Siberia. Each U.S. winter sees a good part of the population exposed to chill risks normally only associated with Arctic explorers/astronauts/Everest climbers.

Blizzards can kill or maim those who *have* to venture out: postmen, servicemen, linemen, farmers, railway men, motorists. Freezing cold can cause the death of the baby in carriage/man trapped in big freezer/welfare pensioner in icy bedroom . . . What is the answer?

Awareness of the danger undoubtedly is most of the battle. Even without preparation to beat the cold, knowing its tactics will spur you (at sign of warning shivers and teeth-rattle) into body-warming activity which helps defeat exposure and frostbite.

KEEP MOVING

Don't wait until you start shivering in coldly hostile country (shivering is normal). *Move!* and *keep* moving as much as surroundings allow.

Stamp. Jump. Slap arms across chest. Blow on hands. Stuff hands under clothing (inside pants or under armpits). Wriggle toes. Arch feet. Bend ankles. Make faces. Pummel. Cup hands on face. Button up clothing. Shout. Loosen *tight* clothing. Pull ears, nose, lips. Clench fists. Bend and unbend fingers and toes. Exercise shoulders and buttock muscles when cramped. Hold toes up for a minute or two when cramped—say on a raft. Huddle together.

Beware of wind and/or rain—they *greatly* increase chill risk.

A fall into snow-rimmed water can mean exposure. Roll over and over in snow. Jump up and bang off snow. Roll in it again. Repeat until warm all over and snow has mopped out moisture.

Don't spill gasoline on bare skin. Don't touch bare metal in freezing cold. Don't shove snow-clad gloves into pockets. Do sit on something other than snow. Don't chafe or rub sore skin.

Once you are warm keep moving by working. Keep working until warm and sheltered. And then keep *aware*.

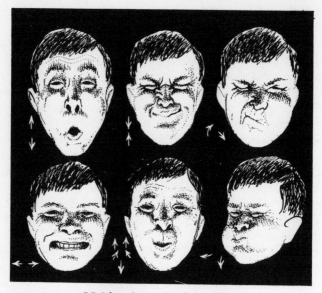

Making faces (anti-frostbite)

ADJUST CLOTHING

MAKE BEST OF WHAT YOU HAVE

Wrap in as many layers of clothing as possible.

Newspapers make invaluable dead-air space when insulating around trunk/over body/under you—keep them as dry as possible (under clothing if necessary).

Paper bags can help when worn on hands when resting. Big paper bag on head (with slits for eyes) keeps in vital body warmth. Anything, like a car-jack sack can also hood the head—heat-leakage point Number One. Polythene bags; wear over socks in bitter cold-wet.

Ring changes of clothing if needed: long college scarf equals stomach/kidney/neck warmer-in-one when wound round these parts of body.

Socks equal mittens; mittens equal socks; short scarf equals head protector; knitted cap equals baby's exposure suit; open-front cardigan can be worn front to back; trouser cuffs can be let down (tie around ankles with cord); wool sweater equals best undershirt (wool next to skin).

Best preheated gloves if losing grip in intense cold are deepest part inside dead animal. Slit down the front.

Head/fingers/wrists/knees/ankles are all extremities which lose great deal of body heat. Keep covered—e.g., pad the knees (if down on them shoveling, lighting fire, treating casualty).

But don't cut off circulation when you tie. Keep checking that no part of clothing—say wristband—is tight. Hindered circulation means accelerated cold risk.

Waistband accommodating, shove sweaters, vest and cardigan inside—so this clothing is not disarrayed when working to bare stomach. If waistband too tight wear as many layers inside it as comfortable, and leave others outside.

If possible when clothing wet, wring out underclothing leaving outer clothing to freeze and protect you in its armour. Don't stand around to do it. Move!

Feet: Good circulation vital. Too many socks restricting blood flow in tight boots worse than no socks at all. Keep laces loose-ish. Check feet continually for signs of numbness.

For long periods in wet and cold keep feet as dry as possible, always drying socks each night. If shoes falling to bits or feet continually wet and cold (and no dry change of socks for camp) improvise footwear.

Any strong canvas/parachute/sacking can be wrapped in layers around feet. Insulate layers with dry grass, kapok from vehicle cushions or anything else that might work. Keep fluffing out insulation when possible (see *TOO SLOW*).

If water in shoes and it is extremely cold keep them on until you reach shelter. So long as you are moving and so long as it is only water (NOT ice) you should be safe from frostbite.

An *extreme* step to make shoes watertight is—dip each foot in icy water until thin film of ice formed on outside (wriggling toes and arching foot as you do it). No more water can penetrate shoe until ice has melted.

CONTROL SWEATING

It is vital not to sweat (destroys clothes/insulation/condenses on skin/can freeze). Don't put on all clothing when working—unless frantically digging in in a blizzard.

Loosen belt, laces, draw cords, cuffs, collar. Take off a top layer of clothing—and perhaps another layer. Sometimes just opening collar, taking off headgear and loosening shirt cuffs enough. Keep cool instead of *hot*.

When you stop, put all these clothes back on—and more if you feel cold. A tremendous nuisance, but essential for efficiency and fighting frostbite and exposure.

Pace yourself. Unless digging against time for shelter, work slowly/surely/efficiently. Take a five-minute break every thirty minutes.

CARE

Clothing should not be jettisoned. It may not seem too cold or serious at time but clothing is never in the way (uses—bedding/foot protection/signaling).

Clean clothes are best insulators. Dirty, matted, torn clothing let out body heat, let in cold.

Mend torn clothing—no matter how makeshift. Stitch tears, sew on buttons, patch with any improvised thread and needle (see fishhook principle in *TOO EMPTY*).

Dry shoes away from hot fire. Stuff with grass or clothing or twigs. Turn soles upwards.

When possible beat clothes with stick to remove snow/dirt/sweat. Fluff out all clothing. Shake/rub/scrape especially before going into warmer shelter. Possibly leave frozen outer clothing outside in intense cold as it will THAW inside and become wet. And frozen dry clothes better than wet ones.

Dry wet clothing when possible. Hang it high in shelters where warm air can reach it. If dry outside, lay clothing out in open, let perspiration condense and freeze again, then brush it out with branches, twigs etc. Fire in very cold weather won't have great drying power—don't hold clothes too near and scorch.

FINDING SHELTER

Find cover as quickly as possible. Take into account your state of health/tools available/surroundings. You must have shelter, whether plastic bag or stone walls.

Get shelter before dark; before you are panic-stricken; before exhaustion sets in. If lost, marooned or trapped, wrest shelter from your very surroundings. You can get it almost anywhere.

These hints may help.

(a) In blizzard you won't be able to think straight. If no cover of trees/boulders/car, dig into snowdrift like a mole. Keep hole to breathe and gradually enlarge space round you. Wait until blizzard abates.

Given longer:

(b) Check shelter isn't in lee of bottom of cliffs and slopes where drifts may form. Nor below hillside cornices (snow overhangs), avalanche-prone slopes or in rockfall zones on mountainsides.

(c) Don't camp right on valley floor if potential flooding. Also risk of temperature inversion: mist sinking onto cold valley floor while warmer air rises.

(d) If on sea ice go for thickest ice or biggest floe—away from thin ice and pressure ridges joining two floes.

(e) Nearer you are to timber *and* water the better. They seldom go together, so compromise. Pick timber as first choice for site. If no timber reinforce exposed shelter with windbreak built from anything handy—rocks/ice slabs/aircraft parts.

SHELTERS

See your shelter is made safe in two important ways.

(a) Ventilate it so exhaust fumes/fire smoke/stove vapor cannot asphyxiate you (carbon monoxide poisoning is common in cold-weather camps). One ventilation hole is NOT enough. You need one in roof and one at door to provide through draft.

(b) Insulate against cold from floor by every means. Car floor mats, car back seat, plastic car seat covers, rucksack, climbing rope, spelunking ladders, sacking, clothes, inverted dinghy, life jacket, pine boughs, moss, branches.

Keep fluffing out this floor insulation. Make as thick as possible. Never sleep directly on damp earth/slush/cold earth.

WHEN NO COVER FOR MILES

Keep moving. Build some form of windbreak—no matter how meager—in lee of dip in ground or slope. Such areas of utter barrenness rare. Make windbreak shelter of stones. Fill chinks with earth. Roof with any available cover—long rocks, slabs, sticks. Insulate yourself from ground by any means possible—even to sitting in or on rucksack. Keep moving parts of body when sitting it out.

NATURAL HOLES
(See also *TOO BRIGHT*: storm/lightning-cover risks.)

Ditches/rock overhangs/caves can all be used if sheltered from elements. Reinforce warmth wherever possible with extra windbreak, roof, floor insulation.

Shelter under and in lee of large undercut boulders—excellent. Build using big rock as main wall with additional windbreaks. Add boughs/plastic sheet as insulator. Fill chinks with soil/mud/snow.

SNOW

Ready-made insulation. Take into account that wet snow is quite different from very cold, dry Arctic snow. Roofs of snow holes will thaw and collapse before morning unless temperature *below* freezing point.

Don't try to build snow houses or igloos—they are too complicated architecturally.

Simplest shelters are best and remember: Smaller shelter keeps warmer longer than big one and takes less sweat to make.

Take off outer clothes when working—so you don't get wet with snow and sweat.

(a) Drifts formed around large boulders or trees present ready-made scoops and hollows. Crawl into and dig bigger. Make a roof with any other cover you may have—branches/cape/ground sheet, say. It is essential to have something to sit on.

(b) Snow pit. Just dig hole down into snow (can be expanded later into tunnels/chambers/recesses if you wish). Cover with snow blocks, or large snowballs rolled flatish to keep in warmth. Make a seat.

(c) Snow trench is very economical in effort. Just dig a slit trench with any tool available in surface snow: flat stone/ice axe/hub cap. Roof with canvas/plastic—adding snow on top as lid.

In very cold climate where footprints hardly show (snow is so compact), roof with "tent" of snow slabs ($18'' \times 20'' \times 6''$) as shown. Carve them from rectangular space (as big as you) that you first rough out. Dig down to 4 feet lifting out slabs. Then lean against each other (offset so you can handle one at a time). If snow isn't 4 feet deep—build walls to make the height.

(Note: Bottom of roof slabs rest on two $6'' \times 6''$ L-shaped ledges cut along trench edges.)

(d) Snow cave is a bigger job but can be carved within three hours for three to four people. More if needed. Check walls and roof are at least 2 feet thick, and it is freezing hard. Channel into snowbank burrowing wide tunnel upwards. Snow can be scraped out or lifted away in blocks. Shape/smooth/slope chamber roof to make non-drip. Chop sleeping bench at height of top of entrance passage and near roof (where air is warmest).

Make cave small enough. Leave a stick sticking through roof for ventilation. Don't completely block the entrance.

Keep everything dry inside the cave. Vital. Restrict trips outside. Mark both top of cave (so people don't walk on it) and entrance (so you don't lose it in blizzard).

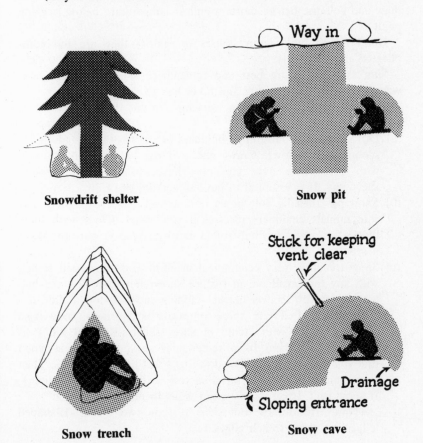

Snowdrift shelter

Way in

Snow pit

Snow trench

Stick for keeping vent clear

Drainage

Sloping entrance

Snow cave

Tramp floor of cave flat. Insulate sleeping ledge with anything going—branches/rucksack/newspapers (greased if possible as they get soggy). Smack small piece of snow onto any dripping part of roof—to stop it.

Clothing might be dried by your body heat. Don't let boots freeze—wrap up in clothing or plastic bag. And keep them in your sleeping area.

Limit cooking (steam doesn't help). Keep ventilation hole clear. Use only flashlight for light. And always keep digging tool, whether hub cap or ice axe, ready to dig out in emergencies—like roof falling in.

ICE

Out among sea ice, all you are likely to have are snow/ice/raft/aircraft gear/parachute. Use whatever best on past principles to make shelter and roof it. Snow blocks, ice slabs, wood or metal panels—all help. Be ready to move at once if ice starts to break up.

TREES

Many opportunities for shelters here. Use overhanging branches as roof of snow pit/hole/cave. Remove snow from under tree limbs, or gouge out a bigger hole in drifts *around* tree trunk, burrowing away from the trunk.

When digging collect firewood: twigs, branches, cones, dry pine needles.

Lean-to shelters are easiest to make—with a fire fanned back towards shelter opening by log or rock reflector. Many variations. Ski-poles and ski framework shown is only one. Any sticks/branches/boughs can be jammed and tied into position.

Don't make too elaborate shelter for first night if little time. Better to reinforce on second day. Build facing downwind or crosswind. Use any fabric from parachute to spare clothing as canopy on the framework. When thatching with foliage, leaves, fir branches start from bottom to give overlapping effect.

TENTS

Plastic bag/oilskin sheet/parachute/sacking. All can be made into tents, whether pup, bivouac, wigwam or ridge. Use whichever best for your purpose.

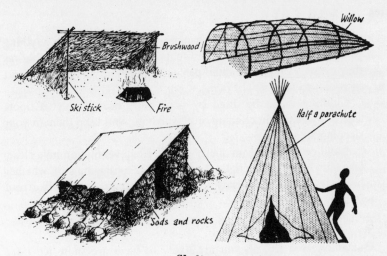

Shelters

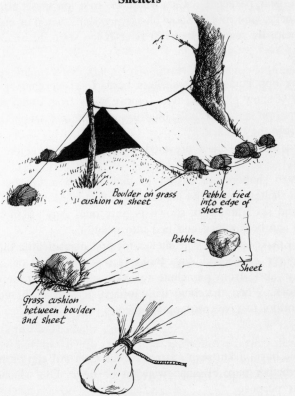

Ridge-type bivouac

Shapes shown in diagram can be used for whatever you have. The "paratepee" houses several and a fire burning inside too—which makes distress beacon. Hooped willow tent is shaped like specialist Himalayan climbers' tent. Drape with several thicknesses of parachute material.

Lean-to or ridge-type bivouacs made from a square of cloth, plastic, oilskin, polythene are standbys *anywhere*. They can be built on flat ground without a means of support except stones. These pull the shelter TAUT (as shown). Tie rocks to bottom edges of sheet with string/cord/laces—which are first secured to sheet by knotting pebbles into fabric (as shown). Stones/sticks/packs—anything rigid —make the pillars at the end of the shelter. You don't *need* trees, walls or boulders.

Block ends of shelters with snow, rocks, foliage. Build these shelters in lee of any available (and safe) windbreak. It is worth *building* a windbreak in very exposed areas.

BUILDINGS

Wilderness country the world over holds many buildings—shacks, huts, cabins, lodges, encampments, mines, ghost towns in way-out areas.

Up creeks, along canyons, by rivers, behind bluffs, in clearings, along game trails, in basins. All offer extended life to survivor who forces way in (if in obvious use, don't carve up place and leave ruined).

CAR

Stay in the car for safety—although not as warm as a snow cave (metal conducts heat out radiator-fashion)—when stuck in blizzard. If stuck for several days it will pay to make snow holes too.

You will soon be rescued if you stay put. *Fatalities in this situation happen when driver panics in snowstorm and abandons car to walk for help. This could be several miles away*—a very long way in blizzarding snow. And beaten back—you lose your car.

If next day is fine, the car almost swallowed in drifts, *then* the driver can consider following the road (even if only visible by telegraph posts) and walking out (see *TOO SLOW*). BUT STAY PUT IN BLIZZARD AND AT NIGHT.

If no fuel for running engine and heater, keep moving inside the car. Wrap in whatever extra clothing possible.

Run engine when it still works and there is gas. But make sure exhaust-pipe end is clear. It also pays to cover up radiator. Wait until the heater works. Then switch off engine for as long as possible.

(a) Never run engine if remotest chance of exhaust fumes, either leaked or from tailpipe, being pulled into the car. At slightest signs of drowsiness stop engine and open window.

(b) Warmth and comfort after period of cold and boredom are likely to result in sleepiness. Take great care NOT to go to sleep with engine running. Always keep window slightly open.

If lock of trunk (or any other door lock) is frozen, thaw out lock. Hold match or lighter flame under lock. Or (easier on your car finish) warm key with flame and try it then. If still no joy, hold lighter under whole key sticking out from lock. Grip with handkerchief to turn. If no lighter see later for help from car battery.

If you ever leave car to go *short* distance in blizzard or bad visibility —as with any other shelter—signpost it with some form of flag on a long stick. So you can find it again.

PLANE

Crash-landed plane in Arctic cold regions is not a shelter but an ice box. Its metal is a superb conductor of heat in really cold regions so . . . go outside.

If no nearby and superior cover, build snow blocks up under wing or tail forming snow house with metal roof. Or make a tent with parachute draped over wing or tail and held down with rocks/gear/ snow blocks.

In cold, but less cruel, climates (deserts at night), stay in plane. Best to cook outside, though, to avoid carbon mononoxide poisoning.

FIRE LIGHTING

It is tremendous to get a fire going. Hot food. Hot drink. Dry clothes. Warmth. Signaling. Morale booster. The mind boggles.

Be ready for disappointments. You may fail. And most probably will in poor conditions. Even succeed in very cold weather, and the heat could be so pitiful you have to crouch over it—and scorch clothing.

Patience is essential. So is judgment. Don't try lighting fires in rough weather unless absolutely essential.

Collect available tinder and kindling ingredients which can be warmed next to body.

These tips may help.

(a) Think in terms of building two, three or four small fires and hunching among them (much more warmth than from one massive fire).

(b) Choose site, especially of first fire, carefully. Not under snow-plastered trees. Not under dripping rock overhang. Not dangerously near car. And so on.

(c) Build fire on rocks/logs/scraped-earth-in-ground—not just on natural earth's surface. Metal parts from plane useful both as fire foundation and reflector shield. Hub caps are great.

(d) Don't build fire too big: wasteful (unless chance of its being seen or chance to dry clothes). Even then, remember quantity of successive fires better than quality of one.

(e) Make walls around cooking fires to concentrate heat. Or cook in a hole. Pots can rest on side-placed rocks/green logs/metal parts.

(f) Reflector of rocks, logs or branches will bend fire outside lean-to shelter in towards you.

(g) Always try to light a fire before dark.

There are many other sensible points: Don't build unnecessary fires. And conserve tinder/kindling/fuel and matches. Never waste matches trying to light badly laid fire, nor use matches trying to light cigarettes when you have lens and sun or sparks from a battery. (When you have a fire, practice fire-friction or other methods in case matches run out before rescue and you have to resort to rubbing pieces of wood together.)

Collect *masses* of kindling and fuel first. This includes very wet wood which can be dried by any fire you raise.

TINDER

Carry this frailest fuel in can/bottle/wallet. Bring out in sun to dry whenever possible. Or any other warmth source. Aim for dust as dry as snuff—bone dry.

Ingredients: woodworm dust/lint threads/cotton threads/dry-wood powder/shredded bark/unraveled string/gauze bandage threads/ wool fuzz/bird feathers/pocket fluff/bits of bird nests/any dust/dry splinters pounded between two rocks/dry shredded bark/fat pine.

Add a drop or two of gasoline.

Tinder is half a substitute for matches (other half being spark or heat). Keep adding to your tinder supply. Take great care of it. And keep your tinder dry.

KINDLING

Collect anywhere. Store. Warm. Keep dry. Consider *anything*. Dollar bills. Family photographs. Identity cards. Tiny twigs. Resinous shrubs. Bits of food not wanted for eating. Oily wood/paper/rags. Wood shaving. Split dry bark. Feathers. Dry-grass bunches. Fuzz stick, i.e., twig shaved by knife down sides to look bit like badminton cock, bark curling outwards. Paper.

Use roots. Innards of branches wet on outside. Drained-off motor oil (drained straight off into ground before it freezes in Arctic cold and you have no container). Birds' nests. Dry ferns. Bracken. Palm leaves.

Note: Never use all kindling for one fire. Leave some for next morning.

FUEL

Collect a terrific supply of anything that burns.

Tree limbs/trunk insides/dwarf trees/scrub. Dung. Coal. Driftwood on beaches. Bones. Deadwood. Wooden parts of vehicles. Plants (like Arctic cassiope with small white flower, tiny green leaves and about 12-inches high).

Upright deadwood which can be pushed over/knocked down/split up (by driving in sharp stone wedge, or clubbing to bits) is better than lying-on-ground deadwood (wet/soggy/frozen). Green wood will burn on very hot fire. Reduce all fuel to as small a size as convenient. *Try everything for fuel. Use in small quantities. See if it burns. Then use it continually.*

FIRE BOOSTER

Spill gasoline on fuel *before* lighting it. Sprinkle it on kindling. Use a drop or two in tinder. But never throw it on fire already burning.

Two cupfuls of gasoline can start a bonfire immediately from a huge pile of *dry* twigs/branches/bark if loosely heaped to about 5-feet high.

Paraffin and oil are excellent fire primers too.

FIRE LIGHTERS

Use whatever method of lighting applicable—save matches or cigarette lighter if sun is shining and you have lens. Use paper/grass/ bunch of twigs to make most of each match or lighter flame. A candle is ideal.

MATCHES

Strike *into* wind (as shown). Tilt match head down into palms to make flame run back up stick if any draft gets through. If matches damp, dry them by rubbing in hair, or holding between palms (head just showing at side) and rub briskly.

Striking match against wind

CAR/TABLE/POCKET LIGHTER

Save for fires. Use sun or fire for lighting cigarettes.

LENS

Try to set tinder smouldering with a convex lens. Some will be much better than others; some won't work at all.

(a) Watch glass will probably prove too shallow.

(b) Spectacle lenses of far-sighted person are worth trying—especially if you can take out both lenses and use together, or if two far-sighted people combine all their lenses to make a four-lens burning glass.

(c) Binocular lenses are excellent. (Remove from binoculars.)

(d) Telescopic sights from guns work.

(e) Try your camera with back taken off. (One method shown.) Press shutter release and hold to keep shutter open. Give lens fullest aperture to make big hole for sun to come through.

Camera fire lighter

FLINT AND STEEL

Strike sparks from any hard rock (flint, quartz) which doesn't snap or scratch easily—with back of penknife blade/screwdriver/other hard piece of steel. Difficulties: in finding right stone, and then in catching sparks. *It takes practice.*

Best to try on principle of lighting match in windy weather. Cup hands. Hold "flint" between left thumb and forefinger, and tinder in palm of that hand. And flick with steel. If sparks catch blow them into flame.

(Note: Best tinder here is strip *torn* from cotton shirt, wound so fuzzy edges overlap and spark can be struck into the center core.)

FRICTION

Very tough technique. Virtually impossible for most people as (1) they don't have practice; (2) they don't have the right wood; (3) conditions far from good. Natives/hunters/explorers using this method carry fire-friction kits with them—like box of matches.

Fire drill is shown. Wood dust is produced and starts to smoulder on top of tinder underneath, which, when blown, becomes a glowing mass. Saw bow back and forth to make drill of hard wood spin faster into the soft, seasoned, nonresinous wood base. Note: Drill point spins in notch at very edge of wood base so wood dust spills onto tinder below.

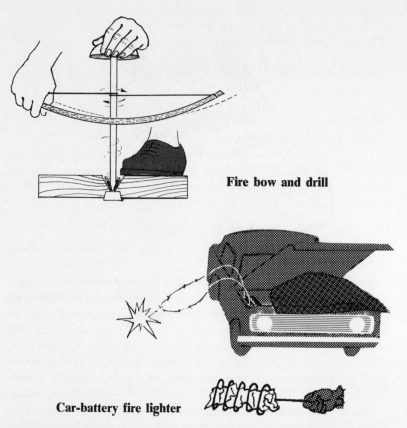

Fire bow and drill

Car-battery fire lighter

CAR BATTERY

Use battery in preference to other possible car electrical methods if no cigarette lighter on car dashboard. Take care: Burned hands, flat batteries and sparks in the engine are not good things. Cover up engine with anything from floor mats to coat. Make a good job of it—gasoline vapor is always present.

Two methods are possible: either touching two wrenches (or anything similar) across battery terminals to produce sparks. Or (preferable) any wire (like barbed wire off fence) twisted to terminals, then looped *clear* of car body so sparks can be produced outside.

Don't overdo this method and deaden battery. It can be effective but don't waste it.

Sparks can be captured on handkerchief with a *little* gas dropped on it. Handkerchief in coil of wire formed into spirals. It should be stiff so it can't droop running flame up your sleeve. Have kindling nearby.

MOTORCYCLE/SCOOTER/MOTORBOAT BATTERY

Same applies.

FIREARM

Little powder mixed with tinder may prove effective.

To try for flame, cut cartridge or bullet leaving a very few grains of powder in shell. Insert a little dry cotton (coat lining) with torn and fuzzy edge. Pack loosely. Fire into air. Cloth may float down— burning. Grab and light tinder with it.

LIGHTING THE FIRE

Vital! Have everything at hand like a surgeon. Never win a flame only to have to run for fuel.

Build kindling into half-pyramid. Leave chinks for draft. Apply your match-fed candle/paper spill/bunch of twigs to lower windy side of kindling where you have left an opening (the cut-off part of pyramid) and shield from wind as you do so. Flames should be able to lick from one twig to another.

If lighting by tinder the glowing mass should be placed in the kindling opening with readily burnable stuff surrounding it loosely —greasy paper, etc.

One way to flare up tinder in calm settings is to drop it (once alight) into ball of dry grass/paper/oily rags tied to a piece of string. Whirl this round the head to try to make a fireball.

Add smallest pieces of fuel to flaming kindling. Add larger pieces only when fire is strong enough not to be crushed. Don't jam wood so tight that draft is cut off. Blow gently. And shield all the time in early stage from being blown out by too strong draft.

Place sticks in large fire in parallel layers. Make each layer at right angles to next layer to give mesh effect for flames slipping through.

Lean sticks radially for smaller fire, feeding them into fire as they burn so that any length works—you don't have to break into short pieces.

Stockpile fuel, especially when wet, next to fire. And keep fire going overnight by constant refueling, or cover with logs or ashes or leaves with soil on top. Take off next morning, add kindling and blow.

MAKING A STOVE

A tin can and heat source is all you need (as shown). Bend, bash and cut can roughly into shape of either of designs in illustration below. Use tools available (rocks/knife/piton).

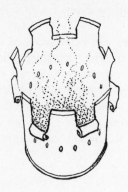

Left: Stove with oil-soaked sand

Right: Stove with wire-supported wick

Heat source: candle (in this case don't bother to cut the can up but make a few holes); sand/soil/gravel saturated with oil, gasoline or paraffin; plain oil with wick of sphagnum moss/rag/parachute harness (supported with any improvised holder—wire, stone or metal); animal fat poised over lighted wick (wick melts fat which drips back onto wick); rubber/wax/electrical insulation which burns best in stoves.

Don't add gasoline to stove already going. Initial gas-stove lighting is risky enough. Let match burn large in fingers then toss it into can turning away and stepping back.

MAKING PRESSURE STOVE WORK

If you lose parts of a Primus or similar stove improvise. Here are some examples.

(a) Lost flame spreader can be substituted for by two stove-cleaning needles bent crossways over top of burner top. Or small piece of stone or metal.

(b) Worn and cracked pump washer should be rubbed with butter/grease/oil and refitted carefully.

(c) Missing leg for holding cans over flames can be improvised with build-up of stone on that side of cooker. This also shields flame when you light Sterno in the first place.

(d) When Sterno supply runs out, wrap twist of paper *around* burner tube in Sterno cup (in a tight circular spill). Close stove valve. Pump. Paraffin will fountain out, soaking paper. Light this and wait, releasing valve until you repump at priming temperature.

COLD HAZARDS

EXPOSURE

CAUSE: sharp drop in body temperature, especially when wet and exhausted as well as cold. Exposure hits normally robust climber/sailor/spelunker or baby in carriage or old-age pensioner living sparsely in cold house. It is deadly.

SIGNS: icy skin; shivering; paleness; lethargy; complaints/unexpected behavior/sudden bursts of energy (and bad language); stumbling and falling. Slurring speech. Worsening eyesight. Looks drunk.

TREATMENT: STOP. And get to nearest shelter (whether behind boulder/wall/hollow). Do *not* press on traveling. Do *not* try to stimulate return of warmth by hot-water bottles/fire/friction.

Insulate patient so remaining body heat doesn't leak easily away. Get him into a sleeping bag. Or onto thick layer of clothing on the ground. Build windbreak/shelter/tent around. Add warmth with human bodies under/alongside/over (even to getting inside sleeping bag too).

Use all clothing available (but ensure helpers don't become exposure cases as well). Insulate victim's feet/buttocks/shoulders with extra clothing.

Sugar in condensed milk or *warm* drink is O.K. for casualty. Helpers should eat and drink too.

Resistance to cold varies greatly. Old people and young (including teen-agers) succumb soonest. Baby in carriage has a chance—if mother carries out these principles: Holds infant close to body, covers with coat and blanket, stops further loss of body heat and doctor is called.

HELP: Doctor's ambulance needed quickly. Someone should get stretcher team immediately. If not possible, improvise stretcher (see *TOO SLOW*). Keep patient well covered during carry to safety. Don't let him walk.

PREVENTION: Eat good breakfast; eat chocolate/sugar/raisins through day. Don't plan ambitious route in bad conditions. If someone shows trace of exposure go down mountain/to the shore/out of cave. Don't wait around in leaky inefficient shelter hoping it will pass. MOVE while you can.

Wear anti-exposure clothing. Wool next to skin. Windproof pants that don't let heat from knees escape. Parka which covers wrists (another heat-leakage point). Wear gloves and knitted or woolen hat. Scarf and layers of sweaters. Anything to trap air (from string undershirt to pajamas worn under pants) vital in very cold conditions. And start out in dry clothes. Note: Too much clothing means exhaustion in certain conditions (see *TOO SLOW*).

FROSTBITE

CAUSES: Often neglect. Not protecting extremities from frost nip. And then not taking action when frostbitten. Touching bare metal. Tight clothing. Uncovered hands/face/ears. Broken limbs very vulnerable to frostbite.

SIGNS: Slight prickling feeling as skin freezes or perhaps no feeling at all. First appears as small patch of waxy numb skin. Feels stiff. If not treated, eventually feels like pebbles sunk in flesh. Pain rages. Swelling/reddening/blisters/sores. And then numbness . . . with blackened, deadened and dropped-off parts.

TREATMENT: *Act* at frost-nip signs. Watch companion's/s' face/faces for waxy spots. Have him/her/them watch yours. Use mirror if on own. Keep making faces to avert frost pinch (see earlier).

If frost-nipped, thaw out immediately with human body warmth. Warm bare hands over face/nose/ears. Push frostbitten fingers down inside trousers to warm by your crotch (or shove under armpits). Frost-attacked feet are best warmed on stomach of trailmate—but keep covered with clothing when warming.

Animal slit down front is good foot or hand warmer. Force limb into deepest part of dead animal.

Never rub/chafe/pummel the part. Nor apply hot-water bottles/ hot rocks in cloth/hot fire. Nor treat with snow, ice, gasoline or oil (all will aggravate condition).

However immersion in *warm* water may help. Warm drinks too. Keep part covered with dry clothing when thawing out.

Superficial frost nip can be treated so that you can press on to destination. Otherwise (when part is hard and numb) you become a stretcher case. And need a doctor.

When stripping frozen mitts/helmet/shoes thaw out first in luke-warm water—don't pull roughly causing pain and tearing blisters (frostbite devitalizes skin). If pain becomes too severe, maybe your warmth treatment is too hot and further damage is happening.

Keep patient resting.

TRENCH FOOT

Caused by having wet, cold (not frozen) feet for long periods. Can lead to amputation. Feet and toes are pale/stiff/numb in early stages.

Keep feet as dry as possible. Clean and dry socks at every chance. Towel feet gently and quickly after walking wet-footed. Comfort feet with warm, bare hands, put on dry socks.

When you have wet feet all the time, keep bending ankles/arching foot/wiggling toes. Don't lace feet up tightly. Sleep with feet dried in warm covering, and raised.

If swelling severe, rest. Protect foot from injury. Lie horizontally and raise foot. Don't rub/chafe/apply warmth. Wait for swelling to go down.

CARBON MONOXIDE POISONING

(See also *TOO WET*.)

Caused by fire or stove burning in *unventilated* space. Gas is colorless. Keep stove burning with blue flame. Yellow flame means danger. Get outside at once. And keep shelter ventilated in future. Be alert to this danger—especially by not falling asleep in heated shelter.

Getting someone from carbon monoxide–filled space . . .
1. BREATH IN DEEPLY, OUT, IN—AND HOLD BREATH.
2. GET VICTIM.
3. IF IMPOSSIBLE SWITCH OFF GAS SOURCE IMMEDI-
   ATELY.
4. OPEN DOORS/WINDOWS/VENTILATORS.
   (Never follow item 4 when place is on fire as draft will create
   inferno—see *TOO HOT*.)
Once outside again lay out victim and treat as stretcher case—for
hospital. Treat for shock. If breathing stops (or has stopped)—apply
artificial respiration.

INSOMNIA

Caused by cold.
Keep eating through day—especially before lying down. Turn sleeping bag inside out each day. If drying by a fire—don't scorch it. If
no fire—take outside when fine, let perspiration on it condense, freeze
again and beat it out with stick/twigs/belt. Fluff out the down in the
bag for better insulation.
Don't wear wet clothing in sleeping bag. Sleep in minimum clothing. Turn over *with* sleep bag rather than *in* it. Don't trap head inside
if very cold, but it can help to put face in top opening. Keep head
covered with a hat or clothing. Pad spine with scarf.
Lie huddled together like spoons. Put weakest/old people/children
in center. If everyone in similar shattered state, keep swapping end
positions (like penguins). Arrange any dry clothing under, and around,
hips and shoulders.

SNOW BLINDNESS

(See *TOO DARK*.)

SNOW DAZZLE

(See *TOO BRIGHT*.)

INSECTS

(See *TOO CROWDED*.)

HYGIENE

Clean up regularly all-round. Use lavatory well clear of water or
camp—and in lee.

Cut (don't shave) hair and beards fairly short: frost-catchers which have to be thawed. Don't wash when very cold weather, but wipe down if possible with dry or warm damp cloth to uncrust sweat.

Attend any tender skin. Clean teeth with rag or feathers (soot or salt can be used as toothpaste, but don't scour hard).

Combat disease with hygiene, and by conserving energy in very cold weather by getting as much sleep as possible. Keep eating—and drink plenty.

8: TOO HOT

Intense heat can spark off a human urge to leap from impossible heights, fling open doors of burning rooms, hurl water on to flaming oil —and make other errors.

So strong is the fear of fire that the unprepared survivor relies completely on his blind instinct of self-preservation. Often the instinct is wrong and means exhaustion/asphyxiation/cremation.

Whether from crackling flames or fierce climate, heat can be kept at bay long enough for escape or rescue—or even while you attack it. But you must keep cool, and deal with first things first.

BEFORE FIRE GETS TOO HOT

1. GET EVERYONE OUTSIDE THE BURNING ROOM . . .
2. AND THEN OUTSIDE THE BUILDING . . .
3. SHUT ALL WINDOWS AND DOORS . . .
4. CALL THE FIRE DEPARTMENT . . .
5. TRY TO PUT FIRE OUT IF POSSIBLE.

APPROACH

Try to estimate where an indoor fire is burning.

If a trail of smoke leads to a closed door, take great care. The fire behind could be small or serious.

DO NOT fling the door open. Nor open nor smash windows. Any draft quickly fans fire into serious proportions. Open doors also allow flames and smoke to spread.

Where you suspect fire in a room, use the door as a fire shield and inch it open.

Beware if the handle is warm. Crouch when opening so that hot gases and flames will escape overhead. Keep one foot against a door opening towards you.

Always close this door on the fire as quickly as possible.

GETTING EVERYONE OUTSIDE

Shout "FIRE!".

Sound fire alarm if there is one.

Try to escape at ground level rather than have to remain or be forced upstairs—escape through a ground-floor window if the doors are cut off.

SHUTTING DOORS AND WINDOWS

Close as many doors and windows as possible *throughout* a burning building (to help smother the fire through lack of air).

Never throw stones from the outside through the windows of burning houses/trains/factories.

CALLING THE FIRE DEPARTMENT

Call or shout for someone to telephone immediately if you are trapped.

If miles away from a telephone (in forest, say) run to the nearest house and borrow a bike or car to help you reach one.

ALWAYS call the Fire Department, even when the fire seems too small to be worth it. Remember—all fires begin small.

TRY TO PUT IT OUT IF POSSIBLE

Act immediately.

1. THROW MAT/RUG/COAT OVER THE BLAZE.
2. SWITCH OFF ELECTRICITY AND/OR GAS AT THE MAIN SWITCH.
3. DRENCH WITH WATER UNLESS BURNING OIL/FAT/ LIQUID.
4. USE PAN LID OR DAMP CLOTH OR WOOLEN BLANKET TO SMOTHER BURNING OIL/FAT/LIQUID.
5. NEVER PICK UP A PAN OF BURNING FAT AND TRY TO TAKE OUTSIDE.
6. WET SURROUNDINGS OF FIRE TO STOP SPREADING.

An electrical appliance (TV/washing machine/iron) fire will die down once the current is switched off. If fire still persists after switching off, douse with water.

Portable oil heaters can be cooled off with water. Take the bucket or fire extinguisher to a safe distance, then aim and drench the metal container and surrounding fire. A SPRAY is better for this than a jet.

(Remember: When going back and forth to fill a bucket of water, close the door each time.)

FIRE-FIGHTING HINTS

If you live in a lonely rural area, you may be able to extinguish the fire before the Fire Department arrives. These points can help.

Act swiftly. Don't panic. Half measures are hopeless. Fight fire with a determined concentrated attack at the seat of the flames.

QUENCH

Water is the standby. Wherever you are, always know where the nearest water is available.

Use buckets/basins/hats—anything in which to carry it. A garden or car-wash hose is best of all. A garden-type portable pump is efficient.

Use any furniture/wet mat/wood panel as a fire shield from behind which you can direct water at close range into the heart of the fire.

Press thumb down on end of the nozzle or extinguisher to produce a spray, and play this around outskirts of the fire to damp and restrain. Quickly return full jet back at any hot spots.

A nonstop bucket brigade from tap or stream is effective. But it is dangerous if the fire has caught hold and cannot be closely approached.

Don't direct water where there may be a risk of hitting live wires which you haven't been able to cut by switch.

Keep jets of water away from burning oil/fat/liquid. However, these can be cooled by a fine spray of water which blankets rather than explodes the conflagration.

Keep water away from burning car engine—impact will dash bits of fire about (and gasoline floats on the water).

SMOTHER

Take off your largest coat, throw it on the fire and stamp or press it down (say on burning car engine). Or use a mat/blanket/heavy curtain.

Act quickly while the fire is still small. A timid attempt will mean the material can catch fire.

Wet the cloth when possible (under tap/in pool/with snow).

A damp cloth can snuff burning oil in a container, stop a small forest fire at birth and smother flying particles of fat from a blazing frying pan.

Sand, soil and dirt are alternative smothering agents.

Foam and dry-powder extinguishers are fine if you have them.

BEAT

When a fire is too big to smother, yet not out of possible control, beating it may produce results.

Improvise a beater from anything handy: coat/mat/branch. Really flatten the fire. Use your feet as well to kick and trample.

RESTRICT

Bundle a burning carpet into the center of a room with stone floor— so the fire cannot spread. Move furniture and fabrics out of reach of flames.

Never underestimate the speed of a forest/brush/field fire. It can move faster than a running man, when driven by a strong wind. Rather than attempting to fight this type of fire, in its path—run. Try to outflank the fire and move upwind. Beware of sudden wind change. Attack fire with wind behind you.

OVERESTIMATE

Always overrate the fire you are fighting.

Check thoroughly once it seems to be extinguished. Pull away charred debris, turn it over and look for red embers. Try to scrape it down with anything sharp—knife/stone/metal edge/axe.

Charred woodwork is always suspect—even when not glowing red.

Feel and probe hidden corners, ledges, baseboards, recesses and shelves. Soak finally with water to kill lurking flame.

WARNING: Staircases and floors are weak after fire. Move carefully around the edges.

WHEN CLOTHING CATCHES FIRE

1. ROLL OVER AND OVER ON THE GROUND.
2. TRY TO ROLL UP INSIDE A RUG/BLANKET/COAT WITH HEAD OUTSIDE.

If you stay upright you become a human torch with flames running past your face. You also inhale fumes.

Anyone nearby catching fire should be thrown to the ground by the nearest person and wrapped in any handy blanket/rug/coat. Or helper should lie on top of the burning person.

Anyone burned must be treated for shock immediately, and taken to hospital (see later).

MOVING IN SMOKE

Thick smoke is a risk to life. You don't know what poisonous gases (like carbon monoxide) it contains.

A wet cloth, held in front of the mouth and nose, helps. It filters carbon particles in the smoke and prevents coughing. Don't be fooled by this false sense of security. It does NOT stop dangerous fumes passing through.

Keep in touch with the edges of rooms and staircases (see also *TOO DARK*) when groping in smoke. Go down on hands and knees to avoid dense fumes and keep your mouth low. (There is always a 2-inch layer of clearer air above the floor).

If attempting to rescue someone from a burning building try to find a partner to help.

You may have to dash through flames. Wet your clothing to prevent it catching fire. Rewet if it looks like drying out.

Beware of becoming trapped yourself.

IF TRAPPED BY FIRE

DON'T PANIC.

Gather the family as far from the fire as possible, and in the best place where you can call for help. Do not jump through windows unless on the ground floor (see *TOO HIGH*).

1. CLOSE ALL DOORS BETWEEN SELF AND FIRE.
2. SEAL BOTTOM OF YOUR ROOM DOOR WITH RUG OR BEDCLOTHES.
3. OPEN THE WINDOW AND STAND BY IT.
4. CALL FOR HELP.

A closed door offers at least twenty to thirty minutes resistance to flames. Remember—the fire may bypass it and not attack it immediately.

Someone should stay by window so that people outside realize the urgency of calling the Fire Department immediately.

Anyone weakening from the heat, fumes and fear should be restrained from jumping. He should be told to lie on the floor while you wait by the window.

Fire drill

Consider alternative action if help cannot reach you in time (see *TOO HIGH*), and prepare for it by knotting sheets together or throwing down mattresses in preparation for jumping on them.

On no account throw, lower, jump or climb down steep walls from several stories up until there is absolutely no other alternative. For instance, the flames may force you out of the window, yet there could still be a ledge/balcony/pillar to cling on to.

A little patience and coolness can save life and injury.

You may be several stories high when help arrives—up 100-foot ladder. Don't panic. Wait for the firemen to guide you to safety down the ladder. Rely on them completely.

WHEN WARNED OF H-BOMB ATTACK

Take precautions in advance when warned by press, TV and radio during a period of mounting tension. Follow the publicized instructions.

HEAT-LIGHT flash is the first effect from the bomb's fireball (see *TOO BRIGHT*).

Besides whitewashing windows, clearing away burnable materials (say piles of paper in an attic) from places where heat rays can strike, the following fire precautions are necessary.

*Flame*proof fabrics with:

2 gallons of water

1¼ lbs. of borax

1 lb. boric acid

Re-treat any materials with this solution after washing. The material also needs re-proofing at regular intervals, as the treatment deteriorates.

When treating fabrics, dry them naturally, hanging up wet.

This treatment does not work with upholstery, but a flameproofed blanket draped over the piece of furniture would help.

Prepare to fight at once any fire resulting from flash. Gather available receptacles (from buckets and basins to filling the bathtub) full of water on all floors—with most on the top floor.

A garden pump is ideal for fire fighting immediately fire starts. Main water supplies are likely to be cut when you need them for aids.

HEAT HAZARDS

BURNS

First thing: Stop flames and cool tissues.

Rip away glowing clothing (peel where cloth intact). Reassure like hell. Vital.

1. COOL BURNS WITH COLD WATER.
2. KEEP BURNS DRY AND CLEAN WITH ANYTHING HANDY (HANDKERCHIEF).
3. DON'T USE OINTMENTS/GREASE/LOTIONS.
4. DON'T PRICK BLISTERS.
5. TAKE OFF CIRCULATION RESTRICTORS (TIE/BELT/ SHOES).

Dry, burned clothing has been sterilized by fire (if still on patient afterwards)—leave. Remove wet clothing.

CORROSIVE CHEMICAL BURNS

Swill/drench/sluice with running water when burned by acids like sulphuric/hydrochloric/nitric.

Take off acid-saturated clothing (but don't burn yourself). Let water drain off burn.

Treat as a wound. (See *TOO CROWDED*.)

ELECTRIC SHOCK BURNS

First thing: Get away from live wire.

Pull main switch. Yank out plug.

If outdoors the key word is DRY—

Dry pole/stick/branch to push victim off wire.

Dry rope/shirt/towel to pull off wire.

Dry newspapers/rubber/wood to stand on while rescuing.

Electrocution drill

RESCUE: As desperate last resort, try vigorous flying tackle so you are completely off ground at moment of grab (current flowing through victim is harmless to an airborne you).

If no breathing from patient apply resuscitation (see *TOO WET*).

No heroics, please, if high-voltage wires involved. Never climb pylons/poles/towers to help. Or rush to cranes, derricks or other high structures which have fouled overhead power lines. Above tactics (for domestic-supply current) SUICIDAL when dealing with 400,000 volts.

Telephone for help. Keep onlookers 30 yards back. Only when officially informed that wires are dead by electricity authorities can the shocked one be approached.

HEAT EXHAUSTION

Kills—and a much more likely foe in jungle, say, than attack from crazed gorilla.

Caused by frying under hot temperatures with loss of body fluids and salt. Signs—cramps in muscles; shallow breathing; vomiting; dizziness.

TREATMENT: Give two teaspoonfuls of salt in pint of water every fifteen minutes in first hour, then every half hour until patient refuses to drink. *Rest and shade extremely essential.*

If short on salt reduce it to minimum—one-half teaspoonful of salt to the pint. Ration it out. Important thing is to increase salt content in body.

SUNSTROKE/HEATSTROKE

Instant action—fan to cool.

Don't mess about when a sudden collapse (in day or night) is heralded by feebleness/giddiness/dry throat/cold clammy skin/rapid pulse. And it has been HOT.

You must stop temperature bounding up and up.

1. STRIP VICTIM.
2. WRAP IN WET SHEET/TOWEL/TENT.
3. FAN, FAN, FAN WITH ANYTHING HANDY (SHIRT).

Fanning will cool by evaporation if done long enough. Only stop if patient vomits. On recovery wrap in dry sheet.

9: TOO LOW

Anywhere is *much* too low when your life depends on your clawing a way UPWARDS to safety—whether from angry bull, burning office block or rushing tide.

And whether it is a mad scramble up onto speeding car hood, back on top of river ice, up into rowing boat, out along tree branches or to tiny ledge above swirling water, the big question is . . .

How do you, possibly paunchy or pregnant, in suit or housecoat (and possibly with crying children), grant your own heartfelt wish: that you would give anything to be higher and safer?

BEFORE CLIMBING

If time allows:
Take off long coat that could entangle knees.
Take off jacket that is tight under armpits.
Pocket watch.
Pocket spectacles (if you can see without them).
Hitch tight pants up over knees.
Hitch skirts up to waist.
Keep trouser side pockets empty.
Kick/scrape/rub mud off shoe soles.
Climb in stocking feet, if wet/greasy/frosty/icy.
Stick adhesive plasters to leather soles.
Wear wool gloves if handgrips are snow-covered.
(Taken-off clothing can be carried knotted around your waist. Stick unwanted shoes in jacket pockets.)

CLIMBING

(Spacecraft mnemonics may help stress key points.)
1. IMAGINE FOOTHOLDS ARE SPACECRAFT LAUNCHING PAD.

2. USE FEET AND LEGS LIKE ROCKET MOTORS THRUST-
ING YOU UP.
3. DON'T REACH FOR MOON WHEN USING HANDGRIPS.

Reaching too high spread-eagles body against rock face/houseside/
wall. Stepping up on feet first, wherever possible, avoids this and is the
answer.

Keep looking at feet (but no further down); use knees as little as
possible; lower arms, when convenient, to keep blood circulating; if leg
shakes twitches/trembles take it off foothold for moment or two.

Clean small, dirty footholds with fingers, nail file, comb edge, chunk
of stone or handkerchief.

Slap handgrips first with hand. Listen. If they don't sound rotten/
cracked/loose—use carefully by pulling down *not* outwards.

Shout "BELOW!" if you knock anything down. Anyone underneath
should cover skull with crossed arms and cower into side.

USING HANDGRIPS

Feel OVER edges (as using ladder rungs).
Feel UNDER edges (as pulling out drawer).
Feel AROUND edges (as pulling back sliding door).
Press DOWN with heel of hand.
Feel INSIDE any narrow opening with hand, *then* clench fist (ape
the greedy monkey snatching for nuts through wire netting who can-
not withdraw hand when clenching nuts in fist because opening is
now too small).

Handgrips

USING FOOTHOLDS

Use anything that supports edge of shoes—rivets/bricks/brackets/
barnacles/roughnesses.

Slot toes in vertical slits by twisting ankle sideways first, easing in
shoe, then straightening ankle. Release by doing opposite.

Foot loop (knotted belt/tie/shoelaces) hung on small projection is sometimes useful.

BACK AND FOOTING

Place back on one wall and lift feet onto opposite wall of any narrow passage, corridor, alley, fissure or shaft and . . . *push*.

Press both hands on wall by buttocks to lever body off wall and wriggle higher. Shuffle feet upwards at same time, to keep pace with trunk.

(Bring alternate feet to press on wall below and behind you—for more efficient upwards thrust.)

If walls close in (narrowing gap) use knees instead of feet. If walls open out, climb whichever looks easier.

Chimneying

GETTING OLD PEOPLE AND CHILDREN HIGHER

OLD PEOPLE should only undertake a climb if absolutely essential —and then only to minimum safety height by people pulling from above, shoving from below. At nearest resting point where they are safe they should be made comfortable to await rescue while others, possibly, are able to climb still higher.

Use everything to assist: belts for foot and hand loops (helpers will need these too); manhandling by sheer effort. OLD PEOPLE ARE LIKELY TO LET GO ALTOGETHER AND SLUMP INTO HELPERS' HANDS—A DEAD WEIGHT.

PEOPLE BELOW: Hold/guide/place old person's feet, shoving all the time. Hold their legs too. Support weight on your own head and shoulders. Ensure *you* have something *solid* to clutch.

PEOPLE ABOVE: Haul/hoist/heave with hands to old person's wrists, then elbows, then under armpits. Make doubly sure you cannot be pulled off by the dead weight. Strongest pulling grip is wrist-to-wrist.

As height is won, helpers below must try to keep climbing so being able to push all the way.

Once aged person is at chest height to a ledge, prop their elbows on it *and hold them there.* Try to grab an ankle next (perhaps lassoing with looped belts) and heave that end up too, so the old person can be rolled horizontally onto resting place.

ENSURE THAT IF OLD PERSON LETS GO AND FALLS HE DOESN'T TAKE YOU WITH HIM.

When ledge is gained, secure the old person (probably too shocked to realize position) with belt or strap to some projecting anchor so they cannot roll off. Treat for shock (see *TOO LONELY*).

CHILDREN are easier to get higher.

Basket someone small by arms (hands using handgrips), chest, pelvis and thighs (legs thrusting from footholds). Child can use handgrips while adult keeps knee underneath. Or child can be hoisted up ahead while adult below (braced on good footholds) supports youngster by bracing an arm between child's crotch—gripping handgrips when possible.

Children can be swung up quickly from above. And boosted up without great effort from below.

If no other way, place child's feet on good ledge, check child has handgrips, then tell child to stay standing there while you climb up alongside to a better position.

KEEP CALM. ENTHUSE OVER PROGRESS. DON'T SOUND PANICKY (even if you feel it).

If child is too weak/young/frightened turn him (or her) face-in to you and wrap arms around your neck. Support with hip and thighs of your bent legs while climbing. But this way is so awkward it can only be done for very short steps.

Instead, if child small enough . . .

Carry infants and small children papoose-fashion across back in coat, shawl, blanket, bag, cushion cover—any handy carrier that can

Fire escape up building　　　　　**Child carrying**

be adapted quickly. Check child can breathe/is not crushed/cannot fall out.

CLIMBING AIDS

ROPES

It is 100 to 1 against your finding a proper climbing rope. Makeshift ones will have to do.

Plastic-covered—or ordinary clothes—line/church–altar rail ropes/ parachute shroud lines/hay-baling rope/sash cords/woven cable/ beach towels/belts/strip torn from blankets/curtains.

All help if they don't have to stand heavy or repeated straining . . . then there is no guarantee.

Test knots by standing on rope or line and tugging knots. Reef knots good for general use. Reinforce with half hitches.

Ropes are best tied with fisherman's knot (if you can remember it). Very easy to tie. More on knots later.

If line has to rub on rough edge, pad with anything soft. Chafing reduces rope strength.

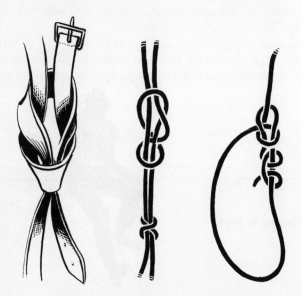

Reef/fisherman's/bowline knots

LADDERS

Lash short ones together firmly with whatever line available. Two 8-foot ladders equal 13-foot ladder (capable of reaching many first-floor windows or into basements).

Tie overlap of about 3 feet. Two people needed to handle ladder most efficiently. Head of ladder may need tying. Always check foot of ladder is firm and anchored/jammed/tied in place. Don't drop.

USING A ROPE TO GET YOU HIGHER

Mountaineering rope work can help in tide-forcing-you-up-sea-cliffs situations—if you have the rope. If you have *climbable* heights. If you forget about the Eiger and stick to basics.

The one best qualified (strongest/most agile/leader/toughest/clearest-headed) should climb first, towing behind him the make-do rope tied around his waist by bowline knot.

At first possible resting place (especially if out of danger), he should search for an anchor (door knob/window/rock spike/tree branch/railings) and loop rope from his waist around it (as shown). If rope is not long enough to make anchor knot *and* reach people below, it is possible to make an extra anchor loop with belt, strap or similar item.

Down below, next person to follow ties to other end of rope with bowline knot, either around chest or waist. As he climbs, the top man takes in rope around small of his back as though toweling it.

Taking in rope

This back-rubbing method ensures:

(a) Rope or line is kept taut throughout on climber who uses foot-holds and handgrips like first man up did.

(b) Better chance of line holding if person climbing falls—line handled around human body is given shock absorber as some of strain is absorbed by top man.

(c) No one falls on rope suddenly after drop of several feet clear—which would snap rope.

(d) Someone in difficulty can be p-u-l-l-e-d continuously.

(e) People don't use rope foolishly by trying to climb up it hand-over-hand.

When second person joins first on ledge, the line can be lowered (still with bowline loop at end) for next person (who like the second did, will wriggle into loop, adjust it around chest or waist and then climb).

Note: If rope can be lowered at outset by someone from a higher position it should—as here—already be tied into bowline loop at the dangling end. And then rescuer should bring up survivor/s running rope around waist.

(Old people should be manhandled higher—with rope tied around chest. Tie firmly so they can't slip out. Older children should also be roped around chest. Infants best carried papoose-style by adult who is roped around chest or waist.)

It is vital knot stays tied. As bowline knot is quite tricky and *can* turn into slipknot, tie rope into any strong knot (over-and-over-and under-and-through type of thing) if you are not sure of bowline. Your own strong knot will look horrible and be hard to undo, but no one will fall out of it.

Such climbing—say on mountain/sea cliff/building—might mean first man climbing more than one short section, each time bringing survivors up to his level.

This means:

(a) First man always aims for a ledge or step big enough to accommodate everyone. THIS RESTING PLACE IS DETERMINED BY LENGTH OF LINE—IT MUST REACH PEOPLE BELOW WHEN HE GETS THERE.

(b) If no anchor on a ledge (to tie himself to), first man must try to brace tug-of-war style behind rock/window sill/tree/boulder/ fence post—heels dug in.

(c) As first man climbs he must keep checking that rope he trails doesn't snag around corners, under peoples' feet, on projections —and yank him backwards.

(d) If rope is strong, first man could have reliable person *paying it out to him as he climbs (the rope around that person's back with that person tied to an anchor too).*

This means a falling first man might be fielded by man handling his rope below—especially if handler's anchorage is not torn away.

But . . . (a) this method needs the rope to be paid out by rope handler so that first man is never dragged backwards when climbing; (b) it needs constant readiness for worst by rope handler who is in for a terrific pull if first man does fall.

If this happens and line doesn't break, dangling man must seize handgrips and footholds and scramble back up to ledge (rope handler taking in line).

(IF ROPE HANDLER BELOW IS NOT TIED TO AN ANCHOR AND IS IN POOR/SMALL/SLOPING/CRAMPED POSITION SO THAT FIRST MAN FALLING COULD DRAG HIM DOWN TOO, HE SHOULD NOT TIE HIMSELF TO ROPE NOR PAY IT OUT AROUND HIS BACK, BUT MERELY PAY IT THROUGH FINGERS TO ENSURE IT DOES NOT SNAG AND PULL FIRST MAN BACKWARDS.)

If first man does fall he doesn't take anyone else with him this way . . . and if he does reach the top, then, because of the rope he has been towing, the day is on way to being saved for those below.

NOTE: When handling rope around back pull sleeves down over hands (to prevent rope burn).

When someone falls, pull both hands holding rope in towards pit of stomach to increase friction.

When throwing rope up or across:

Coil clockwise in left hand. Hold coil's bulk in this hand. Take three loose coils in right hand. Aim and toss loose coils underarm— letting line run off left hand.

(Never use these last-resort rope methods on spur of moment to climb that nice bit of sea cliff for fun—more rock-face rescues happen above beaches than on mountains.)

ASPECTS OF GETTING HIGHER

LEAVING GROUND IN A HURRY

(a) Vault onto car hood about to knock you down.

Pedestrian crossings likely places for this. Can only be done when car braking. Stop legs being crushed/your being run down/run over —by:

Leaping for hood. Law of chaos prevails (see *TOO FAST*). DO IT QUICKLY. Fast reaction is all.

Scissors kick good (uses your bottom to land; one of nature's shields). Head and knees vulnerable points. Or . . .

Hands on hood (as shown) twist you around from front of car— legs splayed.

Pedestrian survival jump

(b) Jump onto footholds when obstacle is solid. Don't reach directly for top of wall rimmed with broken glass/barbed wire/spikes (unless you can grip spikes)—but get finger grip just below and work feet HIGH. Plant one foot *flat on top* and balance up, fingers pressing down between jagged objects.

If you think fence or wire on wall is electrified, test thus:
Are dead animals below?
Are there insulator pots on wire?
Does wire flash in a storm?
Then shave wire with one knuckle protruding from fist. If live wire you will only get a slight shock.

(c) Leap for handgrips when no footholds available. Scamper feet up until you can r-e-a-c-h up again.

(d) If no grips or holds for several feet—and if seconds to spare— build ladder from driftwood/stones/coal/scrap iron/furniture/ hymn books.

CLIMBING OUT OF WATER

Take deep breath. Bob up and down in water vigorously, then give strong breast-stroke leg kick to shoot you up. Grab handgrip or get elbows over side, and get knee up before heaving onto side.

Dock/pier/jetty with slimy masonry needs quick inspection from water. Go for iron bolts/wharf timbers/dangling ropes/ladders to help you up.

Steep muddy banks: Bob, kick and plunge fingers of one hand high in bank; force *down* with other hand in mud at waist height and kick again; stab toes into side for purchase; keep reaching with one hand, pushing down with other.

Trailing tree branches: Grab whatever in reach, kick and work hands along to thickest limbs. If only tips of foliage reachable keep kicking, pull branch down into water and work hands along it from here.

CLIMBING UP INTO CANOE

Don't (see *TOO WET*).

CLIMBING UP INTO ROWING BOAT

(1) Swim to stern, hang on, bob and kick hard until chest is over edge, then ease into craft, or (2) remove rudder, tie loop in boat's stern line and use this as foot loop to climb up. People in boat should move towards bow to counterbalance.

CLIMBING UP INTO RUBBER DINGHY

Climb in at thick end (most buoyant). Hold sides with hands, kick, heave belly onto dinghy. Crawl and wriggle on.

LIFTING EXHAUSTED PERSON ONTO BANK/JETTY/RAFT

Pull their hands onto bank placing one on top of other while you find best place to stand. Grip their left wrist with your left hand, their right wrist with your right hand. Bounce exhausted person up and down in water (bending your own knees as for any lifting), then heave out quickly, spinning around so they land sitting (and facing water).

If you are not strong enough, pull person until at chest level to side. Prop elbows on side. Then swing tired person's legs over onto side.

Use cross-arm-and-spin lift to get light person into a boat. Otherwise pull up until arms over gunwale. Pad with anything soft under armpits and hoist over (catching a leg as it comes).

CLIMBING BACK ONTO RIVER/LAKE/CANAL/POND ICE

As soon as you go in . . .
1. KICK HARD.
2. TRY TO BOB OUT BEFORE CLOTHES ALL SOGGY.
3. SPREAD ARMS WIDE ON TOP.
4. SLIDE OUT.

Once ice starts breaking further and you are in for good—don't panic.

Chances of survival decrease farther out from shore you are. Grip edge of ice. Kick hard with feet. Extend arms over ice to spread load. Try to squirm out. Don't give up if ice collapses again. Keep

Bicycle/pole/rope rescue on ice

kicking and shoot arms out again. Near side, people have ploughed way back to safety.

Note: There is always an air layer under ice.

RESCUE ACTION: Don't go out on ice near victim. Shout directions. Try reaching with pole/branch/ladder, or slide skate or stone tied to line (knotted scarves, etc.).

Try crocodile of helpers prone on ice, each hanging onto pair of ankles in front until front person can offer belt (looped) to survivor and squirm back. Beware when ice starts groaning/creaking/cracking/splitting.

CLIMBING TREES

Problem—to grasp first branches, not always in reach.

(a) Climb trunk. Possible if twisted/diseased with growths/rough-barked/leaning/ivy-grown.
(b) Build makeshift ladder against trunk.
(c) Take a running jump for branch. If successful, swing hand over hand until feet can pad up trunk and hook (by ankles) over your branch. Next—wriggle over on top of branch.

If you need to climb further: Pick thickest forks and branches; grip branches at their trunk end; be careful feet don't stick fast in sharp forks; check for rotten branches.

REACHING COCONUTS

(See also *TOO EMPTY*.)

Coconuts grow at top, so watch heads. Slim, slippery trunks hard to climb. Try lobbing rocks at nuts in range. Or pick small slope-trunked tree and shin up.

For bigger trees use climbing bandage—loop of rope/belt/cloth just slightly bigger than and around trunk. Slide it up trunk to waist height, then step *on it with both feet*. It won't slip:

1. Stand in loop and reach high for handhold.
2. Hook toes under loop, double knees and pull up with arms.
3. Stand in loop again and reach once more.
4. Hook toes under loop etc.

And so on upward to the coconuts.

ROPE SHINNING

Many find this impossible. Knack is to reach high with both hands and grip rope between feet too (or feet and ankles), then straighten legs and reach again with hands.

Weak person *might* manage very short rope climb if good rope climber underneath—running fists up underneath weak person's feet, so making footholds. All weak climber has to do is: Bend and straighten legs (supported by helper's fists around rope below) and reach higher. Don't pull with arms—push with legs.

If rope is against wall/rock/tree trunk climb hand over hand and get purchase with feet on obstacle.

**Rope climbing
using friction knots**

Belt/cord/electric wire loops knotted to rope with friction knots can support a person: Friction knot won't slip down under tension but can be slid up rope when not loaded. Three loops needed—two for feet, one for around person's body. An exhausting last-resort method.

CLIMBING LADDERS

RIGID LADDERS: Grip rungs not sides. Have someone at bottom if possible.

ROPE LADDERS: Cross hands behind ladder and grip side ropes (rungs might snap). Step on rungs as for conventional ladder. Fold arms behind ladder to rest.

WIRE LADDERS: Grip rungs behind, palms facing you. If hanging in space *alternate* legs behind with heel placed over rungs. But if ladder rests against wall, place toes in orthodox ladder style (to *toe* rungs away from side).

SCALING GIRDERS/PYLONS/SCAFFOLDING

Much in common with ladders, but steeper. Rivets/brackets/flanges make useful footholds as well as obvious struts/cross pieces/angles.

UP BUILDINGS

(a) Open windows by smashing glass with shoe/handbag/fist (see *TOO LONELY*). Punch straight. Other hand and elbow props you on window sill.

(b) Climb drainpipes hugging with knees, slotting toes in behind. Pull *DOWN* not *OUT*. Test-shake each pipe section first.

(c) Lighting conductors: Test-pull; use toes on building footholds; don't pull outwards.

(d) Roofs are best negotiated in socks. "Sit" on one leg, foot tucked up behind you and press down with hands. Thigh below you spreads and grips like a tire. *But sit up straight.*

Make for any handgrips: roof edge/TV-aerial cable/holes. Last resort—rip off shingles or tiles and you may find support underneath.

(e) Chin up onto ledges/sills/balustrades by pulling on arms, throwing elbows on, scurrying feet up masonry, pressing down with hands, throwing knee or foot on—and straightening up.

(Beware of stonework cracking/crumbling/powdering/snapping when you put weight on it. Take weight off feet when possible.)

UP MOUNTAINSIDE

Pick easiest-looking way to bypass precipices/snow slopes/ice walls/shale fans/waterfalls/very steep ground (see also *TOO SLOW*).

When FORCED to climb with hands as well as feet—and there is definitely no other way—follow principles used so far. And these extra points . . .

(a) Climb ROCK faces where obviously easy-angled/ledgey/possible. Aim for zones with ledges, terraces, platforms and a visible way to top. Gullies/rifts/chimneys give most enclosed, secure-feeling route but there could be nasty bits hidden in their confines.

Use judgment. If you get gripped, come back down (see *TOO HIGH*) and try elsewhere. Use rope methods mentioned earlier.

(b) Climb steep SHALE by punching with toes then digging with fingers. Stand straight. Always have three points of contact with the slope while fourth (hand or foot) is digging or punching.

(c) Climb SNOW slopes gingerly.

Avoid avalanche risk—see also *TOO FAST*—on any hillside by steering clear of gullies in heavy snow conditions. Innocent-looking slopes over 14 degrees can slip when lying new or thawing on old/hard snow/ice. Test avalanchability by tossing rocks on slope. Snowballs rolling down is bad sign.

More—keep off ground below snow cornices and overhangs. On hillside skylines, they can thunder down without warning.

Climb snow by punching in with toes. Let weight of leg kicking do work. Don't make footsteps too big. Stand straight. Always have three points of contact. Balance with hands (wrapped in anything warm). When slope feels steep, kick steps in zigzags. Kick steps close together. Kick extra-big steps at corners of zigzags.

Make stabber in lieu of ice axe out of anything sharp—stone/spike/tool/knife. This helps hack out grips and holds, ledges and pockets. *It is essential as a brake if you fall.* (See *TOO HIGH*.)

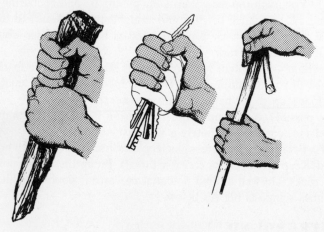

Snow stabbers

(d) Keep off ice slopes. Ice skin on rocks, if only for a few feet, can be chipped off with lump of rock—then climb over in stocking feet.

But don't drop footgear—have it passed by hand, or carry it tied to you by laces. And remember frostbite risks (see *TOO COLD*). Weigh the priorities.

(e) Anchorage usually nonexistent on snow/ice. Only use rope if some form of anchor available—boulders/long poles/ice axes. BUT everyone should carry some form of stabber.

CREVASSE RESCUE

One man can raise companion by simple technique if fallen is roped/conscious/able to help/can be reached with another rope or other end of rope to which he is already tied/if anchors available for rope (ice axes/rocks/poles/ice bollards).

(a) Anchor rope from fallen (or both ropes if he is tied in middle of a threesome).

(b) Top man takes up tug-of-war position by nearby anchor.

(c) Lowers rope with loop tied at end.

(d) Fallen slips foot in this and bends knee.

(e) Top man pulls in foot-loop rope and anchors it.

(f) Then he moves to waist rope and takes in as . . .

(g) Fallen straightens leg in foot loop.

And so on, with top man alternately pulling up and anchoring each rope in turn, and fallen bending and straightening leg attached to foot loop. With more than one top man process becomes easier—but for fallen it is exhausting task.

Important—lower foot loop to fallen as soon as possible to relieve his waist of strangulation strain. If fallen is unconscious or unable to reach foot loop go for help (if at all possible).

It is possible to shin up single rope using loops and friction-knot method (see earlier). Definitely a very last resort.

PREVENTION: Only cross glaciers/crevassed regions when no way around. Keep eyes open for crevasse threats. Probe ahead with poles or throw rocks. Go well around potential crevasse if doubtful. Blue tint sometimes signposts big rift below. . . .

UNDERGROUND
(See also *TOO DARK*.)

Clamber to safety on high ledge above water level when sudden flooding risk in cave/pothole/sewer/subway/mine/tunnel. Or when marooned underground with injured person or lost—*and water level might rise before rescue arrives.*

Use climbing principles. Take extra care because of darkness and subterranean slime on stone. Stalactite deposits in caves are ultra slippery. Clean, wet stocking feet better than rubber soles if you HAVE to climb.

Big stalagmites (stalactites which grow *up*) make good rope anchors /handgrips/foot pedestals.

SUBTERRANEAN SAFETY

Keep pace of everyone to that of slowest/weakest/feeblest.
Don't stray apart.
Keep bunched. In single file.
Keep looking behind to memorize rear view.
Leave arrows (cardboard/soot/scratched) pointing back.
Leave candle/arrow where you enter big chamber.
Move as though roofs/walls/floor booby-trapped.
Strongest swimmer probes first when way is water-logged.
Follow by wading.
Only skirt water if easy traverse alongside.

ACCIDENT PROCEDURE

Especially in caves and potholes. When someone is injured or has collapsed . . .
1. MAKE SURE EVERYONE IN PARTY IS SAFE.
2. GET CASUALTY TO SAFEST PLACE EVEN IF YOU HAVE TO LIFT OR LOWER—UNLESS SPINE INJURY SUSPECTED (see *TOO FAST*).
3. KEEP CASUALTY WARM AND AS COMFORTABLE AS POSSIBLE AND RENDER FIRST-AID. SACRIFICE YOUR OWN CLOTHING.
4. MESSENGERS GO FOR HELP (see *TOO LONELY*).
5. REMAINING COMPANIONS KEEP CHEERFUL/BUILD BETTER CASUALTY BASE/HELP KEEP WARM/COMFORT/COMBAT DARK.

PREVENTION: When going to explore caves/potholes/old mines— join spelunking club.

Always take food/warm clothing/helmets/boots with commando soles/good lights/spare candles/ spare matches/spare bulbs/spare batteries.

Leave word with others where you are going. Explore caves in fours (at least). Check chances of heavy rainfall. Don't be overambitious. Don't underrate danger.

10: TOO HIGH

Leaping from a railway bridge onto a rocketing train roof may be the prerogative of the film stunt man, and whizzing down a rope from a helicopter the specialty of a Special-Forces type—but you can master their basic principles of descent.

Keep cool when too high for comfort—on sinking ship/burning housetop/sagging bridge/stuck Ferris wheel/caught ski lift. *If there is no question of staying put for rescue* look at choice of ways down.

You may be hundreds of feet up, yet only need to descend a short way to find an easier way of escape. Remember, too, that gravity is on your side and can be tamed/harnessed/tapped/controlled.

HOW TO GET DOWN

CLIMB

(See *TOO LOW.*)

Weakest person goes down first, strongest last—psychologically best order.

1. SELECT LOW HANDGRIPS.
2. DON'T LOOK PAST FEET.
3. FACE OUTWARDS OR SIDEWAYS DESCENDING SLOPES.
4. TURN INWARDS WHEN GOING STEEPENS/VIEW SCARES/GRIPS GET SMALLER/FOOTHOLDS MAY SNAP (FLAME-LICKED STAIRCASE, SAY).

Use make-do rope if available. Strongest man pays it out from top for each person down, using the back-rubbing method (OPPOSITE SEQUENCE TO CLIMBING UP). Then he follows down by . . .

(a) Climbing solo without any aid. Or . . .

(b) Has someone below taking in his rope (tied around his waist by bowline) around that person's back, so that if he does fall on his way down, the bottom man will field him if there is still a lot of space below (presuming bottom man is well anchored and using back-toweling method). Or . . .

(c) Slides down rope (tied to solid anchor at top), *if rope is not going to be needed any more.*

(Climbing down is to be preferred to sliding when rope is weak. Rope can be used instead as safety line.)

SLIDE

Weakest person goes first, strongest last. Make sure any improvised line is tied securely—and reaches.

Use: ropes/torn sheets/blankets/curtains/creepers/vines/parachute shroud lines/lightning-conductor cables/ships' cables/bannisters/tree trunks/poles/posts/masts/wire/snow/hawsers (see *TOO LOW*).

1. GRIP WITH HANDS.
2. HUG WITH ARMS AND ELBOWS.
3. HUG WITH THIGHS/KNEES/CALVES/ANKLES/FEET.
4. COME DOWN HAND OVER HAND WHEN POSSIBLE.
5. REST WHENEVER FEET CAN STOP (SAY ON KNOTS).
6. DON'T SPEED.

A 30-foot slide down knotted sheets is exhausting—so are most forms of sliding. Enlist help of friction as much as possible to help, rather than using sheer muscle strength.

Extra aids in building up friction when faced with sliding down:

ROPE: Grip *hard* with inner edges of shoes. If strong enough to hold on with hands alone, do this and cross feet so rope is jammed between a heel and an instep. Once feet frictioning on rope, come down hand over hand. DO NOT SPEED (and burn hands).

KNOTTED LINES. Take weight on knots as you reach them and stand second or two on them. Passing knotted sheets/curtains/blankets through your trouser belt at top helps—allows you to stop at knots (if big enough) and then ease stomach in and continue. Be careful not to get stuck.

DIAGONAL WIRE/ROPE. Get astride. Lie on top. Grip with both hands. HANG ONE FOOT DOWN STRAIGHT WITH TOE POINTING AT GROUND AS COUNTERWEIGHT. Put other foot up behind and hook toe over wire. Slide slowly hand over hand. POINT TOE AT GROUND ALL WAY (it helps to pad chest/stomach/crotch with sweaters to stop rope burn).

POLES/TREE TRUNKS/POSTS/PIPES. Bear hug with arms and elbows.

Wrap knees around. Bring ankles and toes back on your side. You can generate more braking friction than seems possible when diameter not too thick.

LONG, STRONG ROPE. If rope long enough to reach safety *doubled,* use as shown (known as abseil/rappel/rope-down/Indian rope trick).

Place looped end of doubled rope around strong anchor (bed/boulder/tree). Tie loose ends with an overhand knot and lower to ground/ledge/platform/balcony. Be sure it reaches.

Pass doubled rope between legs and around right leg (AS IF TOWELING BACK OF THIGH), then up across chest, over left shoulder and down into right hand (AS THOUGH TOWELING LEFT SHOULDER). Grasp rope in front with left hand.

(NOTE: RIGHT HAND BRAKES YOUR PROGRESS WHEN YOU MOVE IT AND ROPE INTO CENTER OF BODY.)

Walk backwards down face leaning out. Plant feet flat on surface. Keep legs apart. You will have to push down against friction from rope. Don't try to hold/grip/brake all in one go by tightening that LEFT hand—the RIGHT one is the checking hand.

LET FRICTION DO THE WORK. LITERALLY HARNESS IT.

When at bottom and no one else to come, pull one end of rope

Sliding down diagonal rope

Abseil

s-t-e-a-d-i-l-y so it all comes down and you can use again (if need be). Undo knot first.

(NOTE: Anyone can use this method safely if they have time to practice putting rope on and walking backwards on flat ground. Trickiest/riskiest part is first few feet off the ledge. Everyone should encourage and help slider to lean away from side in those few feet and get with friction.)

Remember (mnemonically) . . .

1. KEEP TOWELING BACK OF RIGHT THIGH.
2. AND TOWEL TOP OF LEFT SHOULDER.
3. AND BRAKE WITH RIGHT HAND.

CLIMB-AND-SLIDE

SNOW SLOPE descent often starts with climbing—and ends by sliding.

Start by climbing down easy-angled/softish snow facing out with legs straight—goosestepping. Plunge heels in. If slope feels too steep, face in to it and kick/hack/scrape handgrips and footsteps in zigzags. (WHICHEVER WAY YOU START DOWN GRASP A STABBER-CUM-ICE-PICK IMPROVISED FROM KEYS/ROCK/WHEEL BRACE/HAMMER/SCREWDRIVER/BRANCH/STICK READY FOR A FALL).

When sliding down snow—

1. ROLL OVER ONTO FACE.
2. BRING STABBER UP TO CHEST.
3. FORCE IT INTO SNOW GRADUALLY WITH WEIGHT OF BODY.

Thus, the family man struggling up a ravine's Eiger-like face after his car has slid off road in midwinter can safety himself to top with lug wrench.

(Avoid avalanche dangers—see *TOO LOW*. Avoid hard snow/ice. Take tremenedous care if you must come down a snow slope you have never seen before. It could hide hidden drops. Sliding down at speed is equivalent to rushing downstairs in a ruined building in pitch dark.)

JUMP

Leap only when flames are licking/roof is falling/deck is disappearing/sands are running out. And then don't hesitate—take deep breath and go.

Weakest jumps first, strongest last.

You can do much to lessen impact BEFORE jumping. Forget about parachute rolls/cannon ball rolls/break falls. Paunchy/past-it/paralytic you can take much more realistic measures.

If you cannot avoid jumping . . .

1. TRY TO SHORTEN JUMP.
2. TRY TO SOFTEN LANDING.
3. TRY TO CAGE SKULL.

Example: YOU are in a bedroom 30 feet from ground. Leap from window and you roar into the deck at about 30 mph—a horrifying speed.

SHORTEN jump by tying the two sheets in room together. Tie on pillow case too. (Note: You have no more material to lengthen this safety line.) Anchor one end to bed and drop sheets out of window. They should reach about half way to ground.

SOFTEN landing by dropping mattress/cushions/carpet directly where you should land. A few inches of softness might save your life.

CAGE SKULL with turbanlike construction of wooly jumper/undershirt/plastic-bag-filled-with-sponges. Or best of all motorcycle crash helmet.

Now . . . slide down sheets, hang at arm's stretch from bottom (lessens drop by 7 feet approximately) and bail out for the bottom. Land in a crumpled heap—as likely—and you can get away with it this way.

ALWAYS weigh up your landing—vital if you have nothing to throw down first to break the fall.

Car roof is excellent—has saved people jumping from top stories of apartments. Excellent shock absorber.

Lawns/gravel paths/gardens/shrubs/trees/snow all better than a landing on flat concrete or cobbles or asphalt, which can kill even 15-foot-distance fallers.

When soft landing still eludes, look for *sloping* ground which will help transfer vertical force of jump into a horizontal one—and so adsorb energy. Remember: Parachutist about to land is often moving sideways as well as down—a more favorable situation than a straight-down drop.

If you jump onto a slope . . .

1. LOWER BODY TO FULL ARM'S STRETCH ON HAND-GRIPS (lessens drop by 7 feet or so).

Twenty-foot drop onto slope

2. PICK SPOT TO LAND.
3. PUSH AWAY WITH OUTSIDE EDGE OF A FOOT.
4. TURN AND JUMP.
5. LET KNEES BUCKLE ON LANDING. GO DOWN . . .
. . . SOMERSAULT DOWN SLOPE, TUCKING HEAD WELL IN, GOING LIMP.

(Note: Twenty feet is a long way. People falling only ten feet clear have flattened foot arches. A 20-foot drop can be lethal.)

If the deck is flat and rock/stone/concrete hard, a break-fall MAY prevent you totally creasing yourself. The fall is same as shown except . . .

1. HOLD ARMS ON EACH SIDE OF HEAD (DON'T CLASP HANDS).
2. BEND KNEES SLIGHTLY, FLEXING ANKLES TO-GETHER.
3. BEND KNEES STIFFLY ON IMPACT.
4. PITCH OVER ON ONE SIDE—THIGH/SIDE OF BODY/ARM.
5. ROLL OVER TO OTHER SIDE ON YOUR BACK, LEGS UP, ARMS SAVING HEAD.

By distributing shock over big area rather than specific impact point, you have greater chance.

DON'T DIE JUMPING FROM BURNING BUILDING BY LEAPING TOO SOON (AS MANY HAVE). WAIT UNTIL VERY LAST SECOND FOR RESCUE (see *TOO HOT*). AND CHECK IF NO OTHER POSSIBLE WAY DOWN.

Tell people not to jump when they are crying out in panic and are too high. *Implore them not to until they have no choice* (which is rare).

JUMPING INTO WATER

(See also *TOO WET*.)

Feet first is simplest/safest/best way of jumping from height—weakest person first.

1. PICK SPLASH POINT.
2. GAZE STRAIGHT AHEAD, TAKING DEEP BREATH.
3. STRIDE OUT WITH ONE FOOT OVER WATER.
4. QUICKLY JOIN IT WITH OTHER FOOT.

5. FALL AT ATTENTION.

6. ENTER WATER LIKE TOY SOLDIER.

Avoid circling/spinning/somersaulting in midair by never leaning. Try to hit water vertically with feet together, hands on thighs.

BUT if water could be shallow . . .

(a) Step well out from side.

(b) Quick breast-stroke-leg-action kick when water comes to waist checks plunge.

(c) Or jump with one leg forward, one backward, arms out at side. AND kick legs together *hard* when water up to waist.

(d) Or tuck knees to chest with both hands just before impact (feet and bottom taking shock).

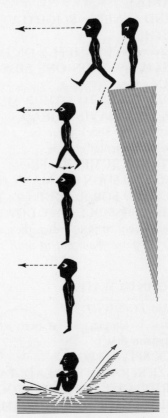

**High jump
into shallow water**

FALLING

(See also *TOO FAST*.)

Fantastic falls (some thousands of feet) have been survived when fallers—

(a) were drunk/unconscious/dazed.

(b) fell on snow/tree tops/marsh/sloping ground/water.

(c) made sudden clutch at passing tree/ledge/rope/chain.

(d) jumped when they realized fall was inevitable.

Life doesn't flash back in front of eyes as you drop. You have time to think MAYBE A CHANCE, and to relax/grab/black out.

LOWERING SOMEONE ELSE

Only lower injured/aged/young/scared-stiff/unconscious if such evacuation is necessary.

1. CHECK YOU HAVE SOMEWHERE BETTER TO LOWER THEM TO.

2. THAT YOU ALREADY HAVE HELP THERE.

Methods vary and depend on how strong are ropes/how many helpers to lower/in what state they are/what kind of person is to be let down.

Tie rope firmly around chest with bowline knot when only short distance and helpers can manhandle en route.

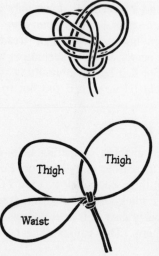

Triple bowline

Remember previous advice on tying your *own* knot if bowline not recollected. Make it a good strong one. IF you know the bowline, triple bowline could prove useful—say when victim has crushed ribs and cannot be attached by rope around chest.

Make triple bowline knot by tying an ordinary bowline at looped end of a *doubled* rope (easier to remember than more efficient "chair" knot), and use the three loops thus produced around person's waist and legs. Adjust for size. So lowered person will not turn upside down, loop belt or line under armpits and tie to lowering rope with friction knot. Or thread lowering rope up inside person's buttoned-up coat. Manhandle where possible, on the way.

(IMPORTANT—DON'T TRY LOWERING MORE THAN NEEDED. RISKS OF LOSING PEOPLE TOO GREAT THROUGH LIMITATIONS OF MAKE-DO ROPES/IMPRO-VISED TECHNIQUES/HUMAN ELEMENT/PRECARIOUSNESS OF POSITION.)

Look for best way to lower. Don't launch unconscious person out of window of burning building when you *could* drag downstairs thus:

1. ROLL PERSON ONTO BACK ON FLOOR.
2. TIE WRISTS WITH HANDKERCHIEFS/TIE/SHOELACES.
3. KNEEL ASTRIDE AND LOOP BOUND WRISTS OVER YOUR NECK.
4. CRAWL TO TOP OF STAIRS.
5. DUMP PERSON'S HEAD AT EDGE OF TOP STEP.

Now wriggle clear of bound wrists. *Back downstairs gripping your load under armpits, head resting in bend of your arm.*

(Prevent crashing through fire-weakened stair treads in burning house by not stepping down center of stairs/keeping to the sides/feeling each tread below with foot first before committing yourself to it.)

Remember—handrail could be weakened/too hot to touch/partly missing.

WHEN TO STAY PUT

When there are plenty of chances of getting help—even though not immediately obvious. On seaside cliff ledge on Fourth of July. By window with inferno still three floors below. (See *TOO HOT*.)

Example: YOU are on a stuck-fast ski chairlift (reasonably rare predicament). Help is obviously near (lift operators within sight). So don't meddle/fiddle/fidget/jump. This causes danger—*anything* that bounces cable will lead to general panic (whiplash effect jolts all chairs violently).

Sit still, swear if you must, but keep cool (which won't be hard to do over snow slopes—see *TOO COLD*).

Many other situations can be saved, when you have time, by the same thing—THOUGHT.

Meanwhile—BE THINKING / CHECKING / PROBING AVENUES OF ESCAPE FOR WHEN ALL ELSE FAILS.

HEIGHT HAZARDS

VERTIGO

Few people suffer dizziness/giddiness/fear of heights/urge to chuck themselves off to the extent they *think*.

1. ENCOURAGE AND REASSURE SUCH PEOPLE (unless hysterical, in which case appear indifferent and *not* sympathetic).
2. ONLY SLAP FACE OF HYSTERIA-STRUCK AS LAST RESORT.

And for people so afflicted—

1. DON'T LOOK DOWN (have companions position your feet).
2. TAKE DEEP BREATHS.
3. GET ON WITH IT.

Bend head of someone suffering uncontrollably from whirling/tilting/fainting vertigo down between knees for *short* spell. Cold air and water-splashing helps stop fainting.

Vertigo-faint case should be laid on back with feet higher than head (NEVER sitting). Loosen clothing. Spatter face/chest with cold water. Rub limbs towards heart. Keep warm on recovery.

Loop or strap victim to some anchor on small ledge so he cannot roll/slip/fling himself off.

FALLS

See *TOO CROWDED/TOO FAST*.

SUICIDE

HIGH UP is best place would-be suicide can draw attention to his predicament. That person out on edge of space and threatening to fall is mentally very distressed. He may appear withdrawn or hostile.

Telephone for help. If not possible don't make sudden act to precipitate person to jump. *Sympathetic handling may get response.* Don't be maneuvered into a position (from where you hope to help) where you could be taken down too if person jumps.

Remember—survival is saving your OWN skin. Don't let anyone bring you down too.

ALTITUDE SICKNESS

Caused by lack of oxygen at heights in unacclimatized victim— say at 10,000 feet on mountain. Breathlessness/headache/sickness. Acclimation is answer. Go down. After a day or two's rest vicitm may be able to ascend gradually.

PHLEBITIS

Blood can clot at high altitude. SIGNS: pain and swelling in lower legs and abdomen. DANGER: Clot could break loose and lodge in lung. PREVENTION: Beware of inactivity which can make blood sludge in veins of leg or lower abdomen—when resting raise painful leg frequently, exercise all leg muscles vigorously, rotate ankles once an hour.

MOUNTAIN EMERGENCIES

GET DOWN into valleys when lost/exhausted/bad weather coming/ night drawing in. Don't make bones about it—GET DOWN.

If too dark and terrain is too rugged to descend bivouac for night (see *TOO COLD*).

FINDING WAY OFF

(a) Don't follow water downhill, nor the gorges/ravines/waterfalls/ canyons/cracks it carves.
(b) Don't enter gully fissures between rock faces.
(c) Don't rush downhill—many unseen dangers.
   Sudden cliff drops
   Treacherous shale slopes
   Slippery grass
   Boulder fields
(d) Beware of cornices (snow overhangs). Invisible when walking above them on mountain skyline, you might tread on them and burst through (having led others into same trap).

PREVENTION: Always walk well to windward side of mountain ridge/ skyline/horizontal/edge rather than towards sheltered side.

WHEN AN ACCIDENT HAPPENS

1. MAKE SURE EVERYONE IN PARTY IS SAFE.
2. GET CASUALTY TO SAFEST PLACE EVEN IF YOU HAVE TO CARRY—UNLESS YOU SUSPECT SPINE IN-JURY (see *TOO FAST*).
3. KEEP WARM AND RENDER FIRST AID.
4. MESSENGERS GO FOR HELP (see *TOO LONELY*).
5. REMAINING COMPANIONS BUILD SHELTER/KEEP UP CASUALTY'S WARMTH AND MORALE/SIGNAL HELP.

PREVENTION: When going mountain climbing, join climbing club in your district—address from library.

Always take warm clothing/spare food/Vibram-soled boots/flash-light/compass/map/whistle/spare sweaters.

Leave word with others where you are going. But check chances of bad weather first. Don't be overambitious. Never underrate danger.

11: TOO FAST

Any speed is fast enough to kill when the unexpected happens. Mesmerized as you approach collision-point—whether at 10 or 100 mph —what you should do to survive and actually *do* do are very different things.

Speeding across the median on a freeway or tumbling in an avalanche, only chaos prevails: Those without an earthly hope sometimes escape, while someone else with every chance dies. And vice versa.

There is no set law—save anticipating things going too fast with you on board by (1) preparing ahead as in fitting seat belts to car, and (2) knowing the best you can do when totally unprotected (given presence of mind to act in time).

CAR CRASH

FITTING SEAT BELTS—AND WEARING THEM—IS THE PRIORITY RULE IN SURVIVING CAR TRAVEL. Yet however strongly you agree, and fit them to *your* car, you might have to travel in a beltless car. Or some similar vehicle. Anywhere. Any time. Possibly at speed.

Given time to think, fast reactions can do *something* to help you as crash approaches a second or two away. Car driver braced so savagely on steering wheel in 80 mph crash (in expensive car) that his grip twisted steering wheel—and he escaped; girl driver leaped into back of sports car as crash loomed ahead—and lived. Such instances are very much exceptions to the general rule that a car crash means virtually inevitable injury or death.

It is impossible to be dogmatic about beltless crash survival. But following points MAY help you survive as they have others (and are backed up by motoring authorities as scientifically realistic).

PRECOLLISION ACTION WHEN NOT STRAPPED IN

    1. DO OPPOSITE OF NATURAL INSTINCT TO PUSH AWAY FROM CRASH.

2. FLING YOURSELF TOWARDS POINT OF IMPACT . . .
3. WRAPPING ARMS ROUND HEAD . . .
4. TWISTING SIDEWAYS AND LYING WITH FLANK ACROSS FRONT.

If driving, hold steering wheel tightly. Aim to get car out of as much trouble as possible.

Back-seat passengers lie (as above) against back of front seats.

This is very much a last-stand tactic. Usually there is no time to think. But with two or three seconds' warning, quick reaction and knowing right thing to do, you can take advantage this way of energy-absorbing capability of car as hood crumples in head-on crash.

Never sit back and try to brace against oncoming crunch. No matter how well braced you are, first the car will stop (say from 30 mph to zero in 2 feet). And then you, still traveling at pre-accident speed, will have second collision with car's windshield/door frame/dashboard/steering column/seats in front.

Going with car from very beginning heightens your chance of survival. Technically—the method of surviving crash once it is determined to happen, is to get passengers to lose their speed over greatest possible distance and hence reduce to absolute minimum the deceleration to which they are subjected.

Nontechnically: *Go with it* (most serious impact accidents happen at combined speeds of less than 40 mph).

WHEN DRIVER IS DRUNK/SUICIDAL/OUT OF CONTROL

If very good chance car is soon going to crash, and driver is acting fantastically irresponsible, protect yourself.

1. Feign sickness and vomiting all over car interior to make him stop. Then whip out ignition key.
2. Lie on floor, in back of car if possible.
3. Or lie braced against front of car.
   (Note. Climbing into back from front seat so you can get down on floor might distract and make drunk or suicidal driver lose control.)

Switching off and pulling out ignition key while car is traveling has worked—obviously last resort. Dangerous.

Make sure you have clear/straight/wide stretch of road. Take a firm grip of wheel (after noting where handbrake is) as you reach across to turn and pull out key. Easier to do this—by virtue of key position—in some cars than in others.

Important. Realize that steering car with hand on steering wheel while seated in passenger seat is very very tricky. A last resort.

SNEEZING

A-TISHOO! at 70 mph makes car driver cover length of big cemetery half-blind and dazed. Three sneezes in 16-mph rush-hour crawl carries him the length of 220 big wreaths in a row—snorting/grimacing/head jerking/eye wiping/blinking.

Stop sneezing in good time by . . .
1. PRESSING FINGER HARD ON UPPER LIP, or
2. SLAPPING THIGH HARD.

WHEN BRAKES GO

Shift down. Pull on handbrake. If no use, drive off road. If you bounce back out, keep repeating until stopped. Use headlights/horn.

If not possible to drive straight off road, brush against side of road (walls/banks/buildings) to give slowing effect. Don't think about ruining vehicle—think about surviving.

Brace as best you can if crash comes.

ACTION WHEN SKIDDING

Driver should try to reduce the steering angle of car.

If front wheels have lost their grip, a smaller steering angle can help regain control by completing a wider turn than was intended. Trying to sharpen the turn will aggravate the skid more. So will braking.

If back wheels slide, say to left, and car starts spinning to the right, turn steering wheel to left very briefly. This is natural way, but it must be instant and not violent.

Overcorrection of skids is common—due to steering wheel being yanked too far over and for too long. Only way to cope with skiddy surfaces is to slow down and drive steadily.

When taxed to your limit on a bend, watch outside shoulder for only true indication of its sharpness.

PREVENTING SKIDDING

Basically when roads are not dry:
1. BRAKE ON STRAITAWAY, NOT ON BENDS.
2. DRIVE MUCH SLOWER THAN ON DRY ROADS.

3. LEAVE EXTRA ROOM BETWEEN YOU AND VEHICLE AHEAD.

4. BRAKE GENTLY. DON'T STEER FORCEFULLY.

Special hazards are: fog, strong winds, rain; darkness as well as conditions on the road surface. For example, overtaking truck in clear patch on misty road could run you head-on into wall of fog again during passing time, with real skid risk on damp surface.

Cutting speed on wet road—especially with worn tires—necessary. At 50 mph in rain your car surfs along with tires off the road on a wedge of water. Even with reasonable tire tread, car is partly out of contact with road for same reason at 60 mph.

Slow down well ahead of hazard points:
Traffic circles
Bends
Steep hills
Junctions
Obstacles/diversions/emergency signs.

Read road surfaces between the lines—certain skiddy surfaces are not always obvious. Rough/ gravelly/knobby surface could prove skiddiest of any. Summer roads after rain shower often more skiddy than same road after rain in winter.

Lightness in steering is good warning sign generally.

Have your steering and brakes garage-tested all around frequently. Inspect tires often. Check with a penny. Insert coin upside down in tread of most worn part of tire. If the top of Abraham Lincoln's head is still in view it is time to change the tire.

(Note: Fast motoring is made safer by increasing tire pressure as makers recommend, usually between 2 to 6 lbs. per square inch above normal.)

OVERTAKING SAFELY

Overtaking means speed. And risk of escalating chaos. Think hard before you judge whether to pull out and increase speed, or stay put.

1. DON'T CLOSE UP ON CAR IN FRONT.

2. DON'T WORRY ABOUT ANYONE JUMPING INTO THAT GAP.

3. ASSESS ANY HAZARDS AHEAD FROM YOUR SUPERIOR ROAD POSITION.

Keeping your distance behind vehicle to be overtaken means you don't blind/mask/shade your vital view ahead. Keep two car lengths behind at 25 mph and eight lengths at 60 mph. This gives adequate sight of road ahead, bends, junctions, corners, obstructions forcing vehicle in front to pull out suddenly, oncoming traffic.

Check in rear mirror for line jumper coming up behind, but don't let this force you to close that gap between you and vehicle in front. When ready to overtake you will be the one to go first.

When it is time to pass . . . in quick succession:

4. CHECK REAR MIRROR.
5. PULL OUT AND ACCELERATE IN GEAR WHICH WILL LET YOU PASS FAST WITHOUT HAVING TO CHANGE GEAR.
6. TOUCH HORN OR FLASH HEADLIGHTS.
7. IF OTHER CAR ACCELERATES, DROP BACK.

A car in front doing 60 mph needs your doing 70 mph to pass— and you must ensure you don't have to cut in immediately afterwards. Drop back if this looks probable.

SEAT BELTS FOR SURVIVAL

Seat belts definitely reduce risk of death or maiming by as much as 70 percent. Examples of ways seat belts save:

(a) Stop your being thrown from car, almost certain cause of death or injury (locking doors often fails as crash distorts bodywork and door flies open).
(b) Stop head being done in on windshield or frame.
(c) Stop face being cut on bits of broken glass.
(d) Stop chest and intestines being smashed on dashboard or steering column for driver.

Buy best belt you can afford. Don't be put off and buy none if full harness is too expensive. Buy diagonal and lap straps. Check with garage for more recent developments on belt safety since time of writing.

(Note: Lap straps on their own should only be fitted to back seats as they allow head to be thrown forward to hit front of car interior if used for front seats.).

It is better to have some protection all the time than the best protection only some of the time.

1. ALWAYS WEAR BELTS.
2. ALWAYS ADJUST TIGHT.

Imagine ignition key won't start car until belts are all fitted to car passengers and driver—and adjust (some cars actually have this safeguard). Make it a rigid rule—even when in a tearing hurry.

Three more points:

(a) Make sure belt you buy is tested to comply with standard specifications.

(b) Have it garage-fitted.

(c) Check that anchorage for diagonal strap crossing body is as far behind you as possible. It should NOT cross shoulder, descend over back of seat and be anchored below on floor behind, as then it is depending partly on seat for support and this could buckle immediately in a crash.

You may not agree with seat belts, but you should still have them . . . and give passengers the choice.

SAVING CHILDREN

Buy seat and harness for child under 80 lbs. Fit to back seat. If over 80 lbs. child can use adult harness on back seat.

Children should always sit in the back (whether strapped in or not). Doors should have childproof locks. Ways to get them to wear the harness: Tell them car won't start until they do/they're astronauts going to moon/they'd better hurry up, or else.

Never allow:

Children to sit on front passenger's seat.

Child to sit on mother's knee in front.

Child to be tucked between mother and her seat belt.

AFTER THE CRASH

Control other road-users by signaling (get help from other motorists and onlookers). In fog, darkness, rain and twisty road especially, light flare (oily rags burning inside levered-off hub caps), placed some way from wreck to warn others.

Only move someone badly hurt if danger of fire from spilled gasoline (no one should smoke), or if danger from traffic cannot be avoided. Treat for injuries (see later). But where casualty must be moved handle *very* carefully, especially if broken bones suspected or complaint of pain in back (spinal-injury risk).

MOTORCYCLE CRASH

Out of the very little you can do in bike-crash salvage these key points:

1. GET RID OF BIKE IMMEDIATELY WHEN CRASH IS CERTAIN.
2. FALL LIMP, TUCKING HEAD IN.
3. TRY TO ROLL INTO A BALL.
But most survival measures should have been taken in advance.
4. BE WEARING BEST CRASH HELMET AVAILABLE WHEN SOLO.
5. BE WEARING BEST CRASH HELMET AVAILABLE WHEN PASSENGER.

In heat of moment you can do very little without practice in doing neck rolls, cannon-ball somersaults and "relaxed" falling. Every tumble is different. Once you are flying through air at 60 mph you have no time to modify action.

It is essential to fall limp—without arms and legs sticking out. *And to fight against instinct to ride the bike out*—motorcyclists with expensive machines, or cheap machines run on a shoestring, never like to abandon ship even in direst crisis. But you must.

TRAIN CRASH

Don't think you haven't an earthly chance in a train crash (rarely as they happen). You may have several seconds warning as carriages cavort to standstill. Further—trains differ the world over, possibly giving you more chance in one situation than another. And any advance knowledge could save your life.

IN THE CHAIR CAR

As train lurches/rocks/careens, and if time to act:
1. FLING YOURSELF FLAT ON FLOOR.
2. CLASP BACK OF NECK, FACE DOWN.
3. WAIT FOR IT.

Quick reaction in doing this means best survival position against twisted metal/flying suitcases/spraying glass. How you fare in full car depends on your reactions. Get down fast—and first.

Passengers with back to engine too late to hit the floor should clasp back of neck with hands nevertheless. And brace.

IN CORRIDOR

Throw yourself on the floor . . .
1. ON BACK, FEET TO ENGINE.

2. HANDS CLASPED BEHIND NECK.
3. FEET PUSHING AGAINST ANYTHING SOLID, KNEES BENT.

IN MEN'S/WOMEN'S ROOM

If time to act forget about wiping bottom/pulling up pants/drying hands. Fling yourself into action . . .

1. SIT ON FLOOR WITH BACK TO ENGINE.
2. BEND KNEES.
3. CLASP HANDS BEHIND NECK.
4. BRACE (AND HOPE CUBICLE IS CRUSHPROOF).

IN SLEEPER

Be asleep—and relaxed: key factor in crash/collision/impact survival.

OUTSIDE THE TRAIN

You can help prevent train crashes by signaling any train approaching crash/car-stuck-on-level-crossing/debris-strewed-by-vandals-on-railway-track and so on.

Recognized stop signal on railways, when no red light or red flag available, is to face oncoming train from safe position and *raise both hands vertically above head*.

At night: Violently swing light (any color) from side to side as train approaches.

When you see obstructions dropped/thrown/placed across rails let railway authorities know immediately. If you know train is due any minute (through local knowledge, signals or sound in distance) and you feel you have chance to shift it, then do so after quickly weighing up danger to yourself and others.

Once on the track (and trespassing) you might be surprised by any oncoming train and not know which rails it is running on. Especially as no reliable indication from the tracks as to which way they are worked.

Don't attempt to lie between the running rails (*where there are sleepers*), but fling yourself flat in space between two adjacent tracks.

(Note: Where ground-level electrification is used, conductor rails must be avoided.)

PLANE CRASH

Take-off and landing are crisis points. Once in the air and emergency happens, pilot can do wonders. Ditchings happen when there is no panic—everyone following crew's directions.

A cause for panic can be sudden lurch in mid flight (possibly pilot taking evasive action, or turbulence) when, without warning, passengers are shaken. Only remedy for this is to be ready for it or wear seat belt for most of time.

Before any emergency (when you will be told exactly what to do), once you are flying read survival instruction card or booklet placed in front of you. This will tell best position to brace for impact. Variations differ among airlines. Generally it is:

Seat belt fastened tight
Chair fully upright
Bend forward with one arm across knees
Place pillow on lap and hold head on pillow with other arm
Push and brace legs forward
You will be warned when to BRACE

Tall people not having room should push backrest of seat in front forward and rest folded arms on it, holding their head firmly. But there are variations to these bracing positions—depending on airline and instructions in front of you.

When descending over water: Loosen collar and tie, remove spectacles, false teeth, sharp or breakable objects and high-heeled shoes. Take up impact position and BRACE when told by the crew (see *TOO WET*) until you stop. Wait for second impact as the nose hits the water.

In planes where you are NOT sitting in airliner-type accommodation, ditching positions are . . .

(a) Brace back against bulkhead, facing towards tail. Bend knees and grasp hands at base of skull (to protect neck).

(b) Sit in seats if (1) near emergency exits, (2) have harnessing which may be crash proof. Seats facing aft best. If facing forward brace as near position given above as possible.

(c) If (a) or (b) impossible, lie braced across floor of plane, or . . .

(d) Flat on floor, feet forward and bent at knees—braced against anything solid.

In each case STAY BRACED UNTIL AIRCRAFT STOPS.
(Note: If possible whip off collar/tie/etc. first—see above.)

FALLING ELEVATORS

It is essential no part of body touches floor at impact.

Many elevators have a ledge like a picture rail on their side walls just below roof. Jump and cling onto this desperately so as to raise body from floor. Older passengers (or in ledgeless elevator) should try jumping up and down during time the elevator falls so they may be off the floor on impact. Suitcases can pad impact.

(Note: All passenger elevators installed over past 30 years must have safety gear which makes this eventuality very unlikely. Worst condition likely is elevator over-traveling terminal floor and striking shock absorbers below.)

AVALANCHES

Never give up in terror of an avalanche: Keep fighting. It can happen on any steep hillside where fresh new snow up to three days old (or possibly longer) lies on old hard snow, and where, if you break the surface tension, it all rushes down like a pack of cards.

This is prevalent in gullies.

Signs are: New snow. Thaw conditions (sun/rain/heat). Snowballs rolling downhill. Remember—one avalanche could follow another very quickly, striking in quick succession.

Keep away from such areas. If an avalanche slope *has* to be crossed try throwing rocks and snowballs first to see if you can precipitate it.

Anatomy of avalanche is that if you are swept down by it you will be swallowed underneath quite out of sight in a matter of seconds.

Once buried under snow you may be able to breathe if among boulders in the avalanche tip at the bottom. But as soon as avalanche stops, terrific pressure is released and the tip freezes concrete-hard immediately—with you entombed inside.

Whole action in avalanche survival is to be in optimum position when this happens.

(a) Have bindings of skis in quick-release position, slacked off in readiness. Take hands out of loops on ski poles or, if climbing, take off ice-axe wrist strap.

(b) Tread lightly on danger zone.

(c) Keep planning what you will do, which way you will try to escape, *if* avalance starts.

If slope *does* avalanche . . . with fracture suddenly snaking across slope with muffled detonation and whole plate of snow peeling away:

1. GET RID OF SKIS/POLES/ICE AXE IMMEDIATELY.
2. QUICKLY CHECK IF AT TOP/CENTER/SIDE OR BOTTOM END OF FALL.
3. DIVE FOR BEST ESCAPE AT TOP OR SIDES IF POSSIBLE.
4. AT ALL COSTS TRY TO DELAY DOWNHILL SLIDE.

This can possibly be done by leaping upwards if avalanche breaks off by ankles. Or to one side if you are near solid snow. Or by clinging to some bush or rock horn sticking out of snow. The less snow above you, the less to bury you later.

5. KEEP MOUTH TIGHTLY SHUT.
6. SWIM.

Try swimming for side. Use sort of double-action back stroke with back to force of avalanche and head up. If in danger of being clobbered by solid slabs of snow try rolling into a ball. There is no cut and dried answer. Ride it out as best you can. But keep your mouth shut (many avalanche victims die from drowning by snow melting into lungs).

7. RESERVE GREATEST EFFORT FOR LAST FEW SECONDS.
8. BRING ARM UP IN FRONT OF NOSE AND MOUTH.
9. WHEN AVALANCHE STOPS MAKE ONE HUGE EFFORT TO BREAK OUT.

As avalanche loses momentum and starts to settle, two things are paramount: an air space in front of face and being as near as possible to the surface. In that last final effort if you don't know which way up you are, spit. And follow direction of saliva. Backwards.

Lastly . . .

10. DON'T PANIC WHEN TRAPPED.

Much much easier to say than do. But fear uses oxygen by accelerating breathing rate and you want to save as much oxygen as possible. Try hard to keep calm.

In many avalanche areas rescuers will arrive quickly. Dogs are used more and more and are highly efficient at finding survivors. In many cases survivors have lived underground, though completely jammed fast, for hours.

It is possible to shout if near enough to surface to hear people, though unlikely you will be heard by them.

Aids to help searchers: colored avalanche cord tied around your waist in advance with marks every foot to arrow towards your buried body (you could tie to a loosened coil of rope before you move onto dangerous zone). It will stay on surface if you are buried and lead rescuers to you.

Also—flares with cords attached which fit into ski poles. Special boot polish for aiding dogs. Magnets in boots help searchers with mine detectors.

There are many physical variations in avalanches. You may be likely to end nearer surface in wet-snow avalanche than in dry powder snow. What may be vital in powder-snow avalanche may be of little note in slab avalanche.

Above action is if you are caught in avalanche flowing as snow, its slab formation having broken up at start. If slab is compact and remains in blocks it is sometimes possible to jump on one and toboggan downhill.

SPEED HAZARDS (including falls)

SHOCK see *TOO LONELY*.

BLEEDING
UNCONSCIOUSNESS } see *TOO CROWDED*
BROKEN BONES

BREATHING STOPPED see *TOO WET*.

DON'T MOVE anyone injured by violence if at all possible. Dragging inert body from wrecked truck/train/car could kill if human frame is broken up inside or spine is fractured.

Never stuff unconscious/bleeding/deformed accident victim into car and race to hospital. Wait for medical help to come to him . . . in meantime do everything to get help/stop bleeding/keep patient warm and treat for shock.

If you HAVE to move victim (say because of flood/falling rocks/ fire)—see *TOO SLOW*.

BROKEN SPINE

Movement or pressure on spinal cord will cause paralysis—hence necessity for NOT moving injured.

Persons likely to complain they cannot feel legs/legs and feet are numb/feel body cut in two. Pain in back and neck possibly too.

Loosen clothing at waist and neck. Warn injured not to move at all. Don't give anything to drink. Never raise head. Keep warm/stop bleeding/treat burns—but don't move for examination.

12: TOO SLOW

The castaway who decides or is forced to move out from desert island/ditched plane/marooned car rather than wait for rescue is chancing his life against big odds.

This is the classic situation where many have left stranded transport to walk out, and few have been seen alive again. Circumstances vary greatly, according to whether the trip is over sand/snow/ice, through jungle or by water.

The decision to travel instead of wait is critical. Judgment here counts as much as doggedness later. Look at all the factors collectively, never singly.

WHEN YOU BECOME STRANDED

1. ENSURE EVERYONE IS SAFE.
2. APPLY FIRST AID.
3. MAKE SHELTER/CHECK WATER/LIGHT FIRE.
4. PLACE SIGNALING EQUIPMENT READY.
5. RELAX.
6. MAKE PLAN OF ACTION.

WHEN TO MOVE OUT

Stay with or near wrecked transport whenever possible. It is more easily seen from the air, gives shade/shelter/materials, offers supply of oil/gas/water—radio. You save energy.

Often the decision is taken out of your hands when crew of ditched plane/shipwreck/stranded bus are there to make it for you.

But travel is often best for the solo castaway—motorist/sailor/pilot—if there is a possible way out. Decision here is: How long to stay with immobile vehicle before trekking out?

There are various factors (see *TOO LONELY*).

(a) Have you given up all reasonable hope of rescue?

(b) Do you know way to civilization?

(c) Are you fit to travel?

(d) Are you certain you can make it?

If you answer "YES" each time, start planning to move out.

PREPARING TO TRAVEL

Don't rush. Pack carefully. Relax and sleep as much as possible before leaving. Test and adjust improvised equipment before accepting it.

MAPS

You must know where you are heading. If you have no map, draw one of surroundings and distant landmarks. Add to it as you travel to prevent walking in a circle.

Make map case from parachute material/clothing/plastic. Don't pack it away with rest of gear, but slip it down shirt front, or keep in a pocket.

Copy map by shading on its back with pencil/charcoal/crayon, then press this side down on paper or cardboard and stencil through by drawing over original map.

There are many substitutes for paper: tin/inner birch bark/shirt-tail.

COMPASS

Besides personal compass, or those in aircraft survival packs, retrieve any car/boat/plane compass (remove any compensating magnets).

Allow for magnetic variations as shown on maps.

Don't use compass near metal objects or camera exposure meters. Check compass often with night sky.

RUCKSACK

Wrap everything in groundsheet/polythene sheet/coat. Strap this to ready-made pack frame (as shown), which can be lashed together from almost anything rigid. Pad with kapok (from vehicle seats) or spare clothing, to protect your back.

Make a small ledge at bottom of the frame to prevent load slipping lower.

Don't carry more than 30 lbs.

Practice using a headboard (broad cloth band for forehead tied to frame top with cord), which lifts the pack frame off the shoulders.

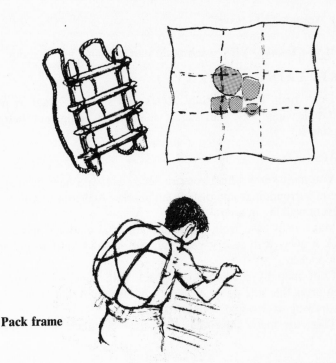

Pack frame

Always carry load high on shoulders—away from hips/kidneys/small of back.

Different kinds of parachute packs can make good carriers.

Practice packing what is to be carried:

Matches/lighter/fire lighters (keep dry)

Water

Food

Map and compass (best in clothing or pocket)

Signaling mirror (best in safe pocket)

Watch (best worn)

Gas/oil/paraffin bottle (keep away from food)

Knife

Flashlight

Spare clothes

Shelter material

Gun and ammunition

First-aid kit

FOOTWEAR

Wear shoes. Repair or make new ones from tire rubber/parachute fabric/animal hide. Anything that can give a strong sole and soft uppers.

Wear layers of material inside shoes to insulate feet. Lace up outer covers with improvised thongs.

Making footgear

(a) Sandals are simple to make for desert travel—just tough soles and fabric straps.
(b) Skis improvised from wood or metal vehicle parts should not be longer than 3 feet and should be about 6 inches wide. Make ski poles from branches.
(c) Snowshoes can be made from forked spruce or willow limbs. Tie interwoven branches in place. Or use metal tubing/wood panels/ wire mesh—anything to spread your load on snow.

CLOTHING

Unless very cold, carry most clothing in pack rather than wear it. Wear sufficient for weather/insect/sun protection.

Don't jettison it. Spare clothing means shelter, bedding, bandages, tinder, string, signaling gear. And more.

SURVIVAL TRANSPORTATION

Avoid load-carrying whenever possible. Use whatever form of transport you can make or patch up to save your energy.

SLED

Use vehicle doors/cowlings/seat runners. Planks or branches. Even parachute and dinghy material. Anything that slides and carries.

A single towline with individual shoulder loops is generally best. On risky ice, however, it may be safer to have several towlines attached so that you can all use different footholds, not just follow one trail-breaker (as is best on snow).

Tie single towline to sled bridle ("V" of rope jutting forward like snowplow).

Small solo sled can be made for long open snow slopes from balled-up parachute/hub caps on spur of moment.

RAFT

Don't be optimistic about a river raft carrying you and possessions without adjustment first. Example: A raft floating on two 10-gallon oil drums only just about supports a man not weighing more than 180 lbs. and its own weight.

Wood is an excellent float. BUT . . .
1. USE LIGHT WOODS
2. TEST FLOATING QUALITY OF EACH LOG FIRST
3. DON'T USE LARGE TREES

Raft 6 feet wide made from logs about 6 inches in diameter and 10 to 12 feet long is a useful one-man size. Buoyancy can be supplemented by anything else that floats well.

(a) Fix extra buoyancy around edges rather than in the center.
(b) Add far more buoyancy than you need to carry the intended weight of passengers and gear.
(c) Don't build square rafts. Pointed rafts easiest to propel. Rectangular best general design.
(d) Use parachute shroud lines/wire/vines for lashings. Strap buoyancy floats *very* tightly.
(e) Oil drums are best lashed lengthwise between parallel poles (as shown).

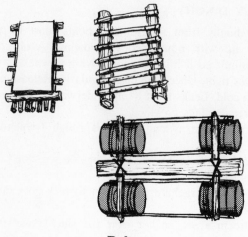

Rafts

(f) A logs-only raft should have a platform of thinner logs on top, but majority of poles should be in bottom layer.

Bamboo rafts are easy/light/quick rafts to make—if you find some bamboo.

(g) Pans/buckets/bottles add buoyancy to raft. So do reeds or straw carefully packed dry in a groundsheet (but ensure folds of sheet come above water level)—lash this to raft like oil drum.

(h) Square sail will power point-nosed raft (more or less downwind).

Punt raft on shallow water with pole (preferably with forked end). Deep water means rowing or paddling with flat end of a branch or flat object nailed or jammed onto pole (say pan lid).

CIRCLE BOAT

Make framework by sticking green saplings in a circle in the ground, then bending them over and lashing together as if frame for *flat-roofed* igloo (place rock on top).

Weave in side pieces till structure is robust. Then pull out of ground, turn over, add saplings around edge to form gunwale. Flat bottom is important.

Cover tautly with plastic sheet/tarpaulin/groundsheet. Paddle it by oar. Practice a lot first in shallows.

EMERGENCY DINGHY

Inflatable dinghy from aircraft and boats must be properly inflated. Blow up with pump/bellows/blowing. Avoid overinflation. Leave seat uninflated if injured people lying down.

Close valves tight. Check inflation regularly. Release air when hot; add air when cold. Leaks most likely underwater, along seams and at valves. Use repair plugs provided.

Rig canopy/curtain/awning if sea is rough (depending on type of raft).

When foraging among floating wreckage on sea, don't drag in sharp metal objects carelessly.

Try to obtain a parachute pack before wreck goes down and you take to dinghy.

Always stream a sea anchor over the side (make from bucket/garbage/cloth ball if proper drogue missing) so you don't drift far from wreck site.

Don't let sea-anchor rope chafe raft.

CAR OR TRUCK

Bogged, ditched or broken-down transportation is not necessarily the end if you are involved in a race for life—whether in desert or deserted countryside.

Techniques for getting moving again will depend on your mechanical knowledge. Here are some very basic examples.

(a) When wheel stuck in ditch: Three men can usually bounce car out without help from engine. Lift bumper, gain up-and-down momentum and bounce wheel out sideways. If only two people—one should drive, one bounce. Avoid wheel spin. Drive car out at angle it went in.

(b) Stuck in slush/mud/ice: Don't race engine. Engage first gear and drive with absolute minimum of acceleration so wheels crawl out. Add weight above driving wheels.

(c) If in ruts, try easing car forward then whip out clutch so it rolls back, then go forward again, then back and so on to build up momentum to climb out.

A scarf or belt tied around tire (through slots in wheel) will often "bump" car out of ruts as you drive.

Hefty passengers rocking car at the back works. Lift as high as possible, let car roll back then build up momentum again until final heave clears it.

Starter motor can get you out (although it throws heavy strain on battery): Take out plugs and use starter motor with bottom or reverse gear.

Drive out in straight line with rear-wheel-driven car, but turn steering wheel quickly if front-wheel drive helps gain grip.

(d) Deep ruts mean a combination of digging and possibly using jack to lift wheels clear so you can place planks/branches/stones underneath.

Use everything to help wheels grip—even dirt scraped from underneath fenders, floor mats and upholstery (might be tossed out by wheels but worth trying).

There have been many improvisations to get transportation moving at all costs. Rope wrapped around wheel has served as tire. Whisky/paraffin/coconut-oil-mixed-with-high-octane-gasoline have all served as fuel.

These examples show what can be done with contents of a woman's handbag:

Nylon stocking (reef-knotted) substitutes for broken fan belt.
Hairpin or silver paper mends blown vehicle fuse.
Nail polish stops wire shorting on metal bodywork.
Nail file makes screwdriver and spark plug–point adjuster
Plastic rain hood binds split radiator hose (tie with straps)
Face powder seals leaking radiator.

More drastic measures may be needed: Weigh up rapidly whether the risks justify doing possible serious damage to vehicle or whether you must get transport moving without fail.

DIRECTION FINDING

You should have some idea where you are before setting out (though to be accurate you need compass, sextant, watch and accurate navigation tables if you are suddenly pitched into wilderness).

DIRECTION WITHOUT COMPASS

North Star and Southern Cross (see *TOO DARK*) will always show north and south—when you can see them.

Also the sun rises approximately in the east and sets roughly in the west.

There are three daytime methods of finding direction.

(a) Stick pole upright in flat ground. Starting in the morning mark a point at the top of the pole's shadow about every hour (you don't need a watch). At end of day draw a line connecting points and it will run east-west. Shortest distance from pole's base to this line is north-south.

(Note: In northern hemisphere base of pole will point south and the other end north and vice versa in southern hemisphere.)

(b) If your watch has correct local time, shadow of an upright stick at 12 o'clock will point north-south. Remember which hemisphere you are in as above.

(c) Point hour hand of watch (with right local time) at the sun. Midway between the hand and 12 o'clock will be a line pointing south (if in northern hemisphere). Method is not accurate when sun is very high.

(Note: Hold piece of grass vertically to cast shadow across dial and line up hour hand with this shadow.)

You can still get general idea of where the sun is even on dark or overcast day (see *TOO DARK*).

Try more than one method to check direction. Once you have found it keep it.

KEEPING ON ROUTE WITHOUT COMPASS

Pick two obvious distant objects exactly on the line of travel. Walk to the first, then, before reaching the second, pick another far landmark still dead on line. Keep in line as you walk.

Remember them when you stop. Rest facing in direction of travel. Draw arrow in ground. Or build rock pointer.

Distances are deceptive. Multiply estimated distances by three. View distance you are covering pessimistically. Reckon on 2 mph for straightforward walking conditions.

Be prepared to detour (as you would *with* a compass) at obstacles like dense thickets/cliffs/swamps. Calculate carefully where your detour will bring you back on course again at the far side, if possible.

Fill in map as you go along to check you are not curving away from destination in a wide circle.

Blaze a trail. Use rocks/branches/debris to make your route clear for anyone following, or if you have to backtrack.

Slash tree trunks with knife/rock/sharp instrument to make a white mark about chest level (so you spot them easily when back-tracking, even if snowing).

IF YOU GET LOST

When separated from (and out of sound of) companions . . .
1. DON'T PANIC
2. STOP
3. SIT DOWN AND THINK BACK
4. SIGNPOST WHERE YOU ARE
5. TRY TO FIND TRAIL AGAIN

Return to site you signposted if still unsuccessful. Prepare to bivouac (see *TOO COLD*) before nightfall.

Next morning will seem less frightening. Try for a high view—whether from tall tree or hill. Look for companions' smoke (you also have lit a fire).

Draw valleys/streams/hills you see on paper or bark. Never trust a landscape to memory only.

If you still haven't a clue make in straightest line possible for a known coast. Or follow down stream or river: Even in remotest area, it will eventually lead to habitation. Continue trail blazing.

If you could backtrack successfully along your path in the very beginning you were not really lost.

WALKING

Leave big sign for any passing aircraft pointing to way you have started to trek out at the original crash site.

Walk very slowly at first. If sign of blisters stop and treat (see p. 195). Gradually lengthen pace out to longer stride. Never set blistering pace. Walk on flat of soles, not balls of feet.

Zigzag up hills. Walk in single file. Don't crowd each other or race for first place. Weakest person should go first on open slopes and flat country.

Always keep together. If one stops, everyone else should. It is morale raising for someone to go ahead to blaze the route and make camp . . . but don't lose them.

Stop whenever you need to rather than at set periods. But beware of too-frequent stops. Try to keep going for long stretches at an easy pace.

Avoid canyons, cliffs, thickets, swamps when you can skirt them, though it may take you much farther out of the chosen way.

Stop in darkness, mist and blizzard. Shelter immediately (see *TOO COLD*).

Always stop in good time to prepare camp before darkness.

Negotiate unpassable swamps with pole. If sinking, lie flat and roll and wriggle with pole crosswise under shoulders or chest to "swim" to side. Don't make violent panicky movements.

Keep eating (see *TOO EMPTY*), drinking (see *TOO DRY*) and cheerful: Sing.

SLEDDING

Don't be tempted to ride *fast* down steep slopes on sled after long session of hauling.

Sit astride small sled with feet firmly planted on ground. And grasping line at front. Brake by digging in heels and lifting front end of sled off the ground.

Pick clear route to bottom—well away from trees which are hard to steer through. Keep braking.

CARRYING SOMEONE INJURED

Lifting a casualty to a safe place for treatment *anywhere* needs improvisation and patience. There are various methods.

(a) Fireman's lift (as shown)
(b) Two-, three- and four-handed lifts (as shown)
(c) Sheet slid on level floor (as shown)
(d) Coat-and-poles stretcher (as shown)
(e) Rope stretcher—hard to make and carry
(f) Piggyback with victim's feet through a rucksack frame (worn on carrier's back): Suitable when the injured can hang on to you
(g) Same as above with injured's feet slipped through coil of rope, coil being worn by carrier like a coat (he first puts one arm through it, then the other and top of coil crosses back of his neck)
(h) Sled as carrier—don't speed
(i) Raft carrier—be careful not to capsize.

Don't cripple yourself trying to fireman's lift someone too heavy. You need additional help. Remember principles of lifting—see *TOO LONELY*.

Fireman's lift

Three-handed lift

Four- and two-handed lifts

When injured is not in desperate-looking condition and HAS to be moved to safety he/she can be carried between two helpers using various handgrips. Three-handed one is variation on two-handed (see below), depending on weight/strength/size of injured and helpers. Injured is supported by free hand of one helper.

Four-handed lift can carry injured who is able to hold on to shoulders of two people carrying him between them. Two-hand grip (note handkerchief for comfort) is best for injured not able to help himself at all—and who is then supported by both carriers' spare arms in position roughly as for three-handed lift (above).

Serious casualties should be moved as little as possible (see *TOO FAST*). If essential, however, move on improvised stretcher for patient must be in lying or semilying position. Best stretcher is rigid—door/plank/bench. Failing this use jackets and coats threaded on poles as shown.

Makeshift stretcher

If possible to drag injured just a short way to safety, feed blanket/sheet/tarpaulin underneath (very gently) keeping body in position it already lies.

Remember . . .

1. MOVE BODY LENGTHWAYS NOT SIDEWAYS, and if you have to *lift* patient (heaven forbid), then support *each part of body and carry it in a straight line* . . .
2. NEVER LET BODY SAG IN CENTER BY JUST PICKING UP HEAD AND FEET.

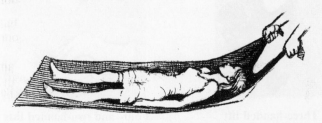

Drag sheet

WATER TRAVEL

CROSSING RIVERS

(See *TOO WET* .)

RAFTING

Distribute weight over raft evenly. Stand or sit around edges to balance other paddlers. If load slips, balance it on far side immediately while sorting it out.

A sail can be more trouble than it's worth. But if your course is downwind take advantage of it.

Raft travel is very slow. Take it easy. Don't try to hurry. Only sail in daylight. Don't fall asleep. Listen and watch for hazards ahead: spray/noise/silver line across water. Don't enter smooth-walled gorges. Attach a long line so you can let raft down small river rapids from the bank.

Keep near to land. When faced with rough water, carry gear around and float your raft down rapids (on its rope) or build another raft at the bottom.

Always lift raft high onto river bank at night and unload the gear. Beware of flooding during a sudden storm.

DINGHY SURVIVAL

Avoid leaping into dinghy after ditching or boat wreck. Climb in carefully.

1. CHECK EVERYONE IS ABOARD
2. PADDLE AWAY FROM SINKING WRECK
3. JOIN UP WITH OTHER DINGHIES
4. PUT OUT SEA ANCHOR
5. APPLY FIRST AID

Dinghies should link together with 25-foot lines: tie stern of first boat to bow of second and so on. Keep sea-anchor line long, and if you lose this anchor substitute a makeshift one at once to stop you from drifting away.

Generally aim to stay near crisis site for three days at least for best chance of rescue. During this time:

(a) Retrieve stores/wreckage/buoyancy floating around (but beware sharp metal bits which could puncture dinghy floor and buoyancy chamber).
(b) Shelter from bad weather with whatever cover dinghy affords.
(c) Keep watch in two-hour stands. Tie person on duty to boat with 20-foot line. He should inspect boat for leaks. Keep bailing. Watch for chance of rescue.
(d) Have signaling gear ready to use immediately.
(e) Ration water and food. Set out solar stills.

Only try to move dinghy out of crisis area if land definitely in reach or sharks attracted by floating food/bodies/remains.

Don't try to sail dinghy unless land is near and downwind. Make sail from anything handy. Inflate boat fully, take in sea anchor and use oar as rudder. Don't secure bottom of sail but hold it with hand-held line so sudden gust doesn't capsize you.

Avoid capsizal (see *TOO WET*) by sitting low in boat in rough weather, keeping sea anchor out, and distributing everyone to ballast the weather side. Don't sit on sides or stand up. When you move warn the others.

Signs of land sometimes are:

Cumulus cloud stationary in clear sky
Green tint in sky above lagoon
Drifting wood
White sky above snow fields (water makes for gray sky)
Lighter color of water
Roar of surf
Continued bird cries
Bird-flight direction in early morning and sunset

If you arrive off land at night, wait until morning to beach if possible. Then select landing point very carefully.

Go to lee of island or point of land. Don't land with sun in your eyes. Steer clear of rocks/reefs/wrecks.

Make for clear gaps in surf. Sloping beach with small surf is ideal. Try to ride on back of breaker, paddling hard.

Big surf means keeping on clothes and shoes, checking life jackets; streaming out sea anchor on as long a line as possible (and keeping strain on anchor by adjusting); all hands at the paddles.

Sea anchor will keep you pointing at the shore. Paddle hard to get through oncoming crest and avoid being swept broadside. Try to hold dinghy back from overshooting back of breaker.

Seize raft if you capsize (see *TOO WET*).

DRIVING

SNOW/ICE/SLUSH

Drive slowly, gently and in a higher gear than usual. Take hill in top which you would normally climb in third.

Be alert to lightness of steering. If you have to brake do it on the straight. Pump brakes gently instead of hitting them. Release brakes if you skid (see *TOO FAST*).

Keep normal tire inflation on snow. Keep as much weight as possible over driving wheels and stop as little as possible.

Wait until you have a clear run uphill. Avoid trying to climb in too low a gear: Overrevving causes wheel spin. Avoid steep hills where possible.

On banked curves (say on hairpins) where car might slide over edge, travel with wheels on shoulder or in gutter of far side of any drop.

If wheels start spinning on hill climb, passengers should try jumping up and down inside.

Select low gear to go downhill. Use brakes gently. On very dangerous slopes descend with engine in lowest gear.

If trapped in snow—(see *TOO COLD*).

THROUGH WATER

Inspect water to see if too deep (height of distributor and carburetor decide this).

(Note: An exhaust pipe extension is useful but not essential.)

Remove fan belt if a lot of water ahead—to stop fan blades drenching engine.

Stop and cool the engine before starting. Then close windows and start through at 3 mph. Avoid a bow wave piling up against front of car.

Don't burn out the clutch. Avoid stalling the engine.

Passengers should be ready to jump out and push if wheels start spinning.

A sheet of water ahead can make it impossible to see limits of roadside: You may be driving straight for a river (see *TOO WET*). Watch sides of road when you first inspect water.

Hedges indicate road, but never trust telegraph poles—they may cut across country. Watch ripples from car. They change formation when passing over submerged drop-off.

If water swamps car electrical circuits, try this long shot: Pull choke (if car has one) right out and fire engine in the hope you can get one cylinder working. If this happens push choke home and keep engine going (in neutral). Eventually other cylinders will join in.

Usually you have to get out and dry leads and distributor with dry cloth. But wait ten minutes first to let stored-in engine heat do some of the drying too.

MUD

Avoid wheel spin. Place weight over the driving wheels. Bad patches can be prepared in advance by laying rocks/foliage/sacks. Press accelerator pedal lightly.

Don't stop once moving. If wheels start spinning don't rev but reverse quickly.

MOUNTAIN PASS

Change down in good time for steep gradients. Don't overrev on hairpins. Choose the easiest line of a very sharp corner—around outside edge.

If radiator boils, switch off engine. Sometimes you can turn car to face the wind. Or freewheel down other side if top already reached. Fill up radiator when cool.

If losing power and failing to climb—try ascent in reverse.

Vapor lock in fuel supply (due to overheating) is cured if you: 1. Allow engine to cool. 2. Apply wet cloth to fuel-system parts. 3. Prime carburetor by hand.

SAND

Drifts could cover desert tracks.

Keep going at all costs when moving on soft sand until you reach hard ground. Avoid wheel spin (but you may have to change down to first gear as more chance of stalling in top gear).

Don't stop if engine boils until that hard patch of ground is reached.

If stuck: Dig and use jack to slide sand tracks (metal channels/ wire mesh/rocks) under wheels.

Sandstorm can be seen approaching. You may be able to drive around it. If no escape: Face vehicle away from storm, seal it as well as you can against sand and drive it onto sand tracks.

Wait until storm stops. Don't try to leave vehicle.

ASPECTS OF TRAVEL

ARCTIC

Travel is extremely strenuous (see *TOO COLD*).

Salvage gear from aircraft or boat as soon as risk of fire from crash/ditching/landing has passed. Drain oil before it freezes. Remove battery and keep warm. See to clothing/shelter/fire.

Prepare signaling gear while waiting for rescue (see *TOO LONELY*).

If you decide to move out, head for coast/major river/settlement.

Snowshoes or skis are essential—especially in timber country. Try to travel by river: on raft or dinghy in summer, on ice in winter. But if river very twisting avoid by taking to higher ground ridges.

Keep to inside of bends on river ice. Walk on the far side of junction where rivers meet. Or travel by land until well downriver of the junction. Beware of thin ice all the time.

Check on your tracks behind to help keep on route. Walk 30 paces apart in single file so last man can line up those ahead with compass or by eye to ensure straight traveling in absence of obvious landmarks.

Avoid swamps/tundra lakes/quicksand. But dig into snow and shelter in face of coming blizzard.

Don't leave anyone behind on sea ice. Distant landmarks of ice unreliable for direction-finding as they move. Be ready for ice to break up, ice floes to prove unstable, icebergs to capsize. Keep checking compass (unreliable here) with stars.

Actual texture of ice varies according to season. Shelter on low-lying, level-topped ice. Don't make rash jumps across water from extreme edges of ice—always leap with about 2 feet to spare.

DESERT

A huge area offering very arduous travel (see *TOO DRY*).

Immediate action: Take water from transport; wait until any fire risk from immobilized transportation passes; salvage rest of survival gear; relax.

It is vital not to panic and rush in desert heat. Lie in shade and make plans. You should attempt to stay put for at least seven days.

Travel is likely to be over hilly country with unexpected weather changes: windy/freezing/foggy as well as simmering. You should not carry more than 30 lbs. weight, yet 1 gallon of water weighs 10 lbs. (Hence the travel risk.)

If some stay and some travel, those walking should take more water than those left awaiting for rescue: How much depends on water supply.

Travelers carry water mainly (plus piece of parachute/groundsheet/polythene for shade, clothing, a little food, and navigation aids). Remember flashlight as you should travel only at night.

(Note: In winter there will be opportunities to travel through days.)

Rest during hot days under double thickness of shelter material rigged bivouac-style (see *TOO COLD*). Remove shoes and socks when resting (and clean frequently of sand).

Take whatever cover is available in a sandstorm. Button up clothing. If caught in open, lie on ground facing away. Roll occasionally to avoid being buried.

Walk on ridges or troughs between dunes. Steer clear of soft sand where possible. Take care traveling in the dark—sudden slopes are steeper than they look. Develop your night vision.

You must plan route to definite destination. Once you have made a decision don't change it. Set out for road or coast if possible rather than pinpoint a village/oasis/settlement—unless very near.

JUNGLE

Travel is exacting, but necessary, as tree canopy conceals you from any air search and masks your signals. Ferocious animals, giant spiders, huge snakes and savages are nowhere nearly as dangerous as . . .

Heat exhaustion (see *TOO HOT*)

Sickness/fever/poisoning (see *TOO CROWDED/TOO EMPTY*)

Panic (see *TOO LONELY*)

Cross-country travel very difficult. Follow rivers (both wet and dry), game trails, native paths, ridges. But never follow water too closely downhill as it takes shortest route down waterfalls/defiles/gullies.

When you find a trail—follow it. Good places for this: river crossings; low hill passes; river rapids. You may see natives here (see *TOO CROWDED*). Native villages are sited on stream banks.

Main jungle equipment—water (refill containers whenever possible), machete or knife, compass, strong shoes, hammock and shelter, first-aid kit.

Trust compass more than maps. Check it with night sky. Sun rises too high in day to be accurate guide, except early in morning and late afternoon. Follow water when without compass.

Detour any dense foliage/swamps/ravines. Don't travel at night when trails mentioned above are used by animals and reptiles. Always take easiest line.

You are soaked with rain and sweat in jungle. Body moisture and vital salts are lost. Keep drinking (and taking salt). Defy heat exhaustion (see *TOO HOT*).

If separated from companions bang a stick against tree trunks—the noise carries farther than shouting. Take action if lost and separated from companions (see earlier). But this should never happen. Stick together.

Watch for trees with octopus-like roots and avoid swamps they indicate. Also beware of falling deadwood/coconuts/animals by looking up often.

Make plenty of noise to warn animals (like beating on trunks). Travel in single file with front man breaking trail with machete or knife.

Avoid rotting logs/stumps/branches—they harbor ticks. Beware of crocodile risk when faced with water. Don't blunder into hornet's nest. Be alert.

Rest often. And stop well before dark to make camp.

(a) Choose solid ground, not marshy. Avoid deadwood above you. Check flooding risk. Clear ground completely of vegetation.

(b) Sleep off ground in hammock or on raised bed of branches and leaves. Simplest design resembles small four-poster bed with parachute canopy completely draped over. Simple bivouac shelter (see *TOO COLD*) is good general shelter too.

Bivouac and hammock

(c) Build thorn fence around camp if uneasy. Keep fire lit all night. Wrap up well against cold.

(d) Scatter ash from fire around camp to stop insects crawling in.

Any amount of improvisation can be carried out with wood and huge leaves in jungle with knife or sharp stones. Leaves are a good shelter thatch. Bamboo makes fishhooks/harpoons/furniture. Ferns, vines, canes, weeds and flowers can often produce string/twine/cord.

MOUNTAIN

Avoid mountain ranges when possible (see *TOO HIGH/TOO LOW/TOO COLD*). Especially when snow-capped and presenting glaciers and avalanche possibilities.

If no rope, no ice axe for each person, no experienced leader give a wide berth. If no alternative: Travel in early morning when snow and ice are frozen hard. Beware once sun starts to melt slopes.

TRAVEL HAZARDS

FROSTBITE	
EXPOSURE	see *TOO COLD*
TRENCH FOOT	
HEAT EXHAUSTION	see *TOO HOT*
SUNSTROKE	
SUNBLINDNESS	see *TOO BRIGHT*
SUNBURN	

BLISTERS

Don't break foot blisters. As soon as skin reddens apply a Band-Aid (if available). Edges can be pricked with flame-sterilized point. Press fluid out gently. Dry with improvised bandage. If very painful rest until better.

Prevention: Wash/rinse/dry socks each night. Darn holes immediately (and artfully). Always keep change of socks if possible.

Hot salt-water bath is comforting.

RASHES

Soothe irritation from poisonous plants with—if nothing else—coconut oil, or paste of wood ash and water. Bandage.

A good tan (gained under hot sun from only five minutes exposure daily) is best protection against prickly heat and sunburn.

SEASICKNESS

Concentrate on some job. If possible try to eat small light snacks. Lie still, keep changing head position. Keep warm. Take seasickness tablets if available.

SALT-WATER SORES

Keep body as dry as possible. Don't open or squeeze sores. Clean gently. Cover large sores with dressing. Antiseptic cream O.K. if you have it.

CONSTIPATION

Expect it when short on food and water. Don't use laxatives—and rob body of moisture. Also expect dark urine (difficult to pass). Don't worry about it.

CRACKED LIPS/PARCHED SKIN

Use oil/salve/chapstick or any sun cream—if handy.

13: TOO FULL

The exploding bomb fills the atmosphere with flash and fire, blast and radiation fallout. What can anyone do in the face of such destruction?

Nothing you have not done already. It is by advance preparations that you might survive, no matter how helpless you feel. These preparations would definitely save life.

No one is immune from or necessarily doomed by nuclear-bomb attack (it could miss a target to hit theoretically safe ground). Take precautions on the chance you are outside the explosion area.

BOMB EFFECTS

FLASH-HEAT

(See *TOO BRIGHT/TOO HOT.*)

BLAST

Like thunder follows lightning, blast follows flash—almost immediately or possibly over a minute later. The force will uproot trees/flatten buildings/make people into missiles in the devastation area. And still wreak damage outside it.

RADIATION FALLOUT

The explosion churns wreckage into dust which is sucked up into the fireball—and then released as deadly contaminated dust. Every bit dropping back is radioactive.

Fallout will fill the explosion area within an hour and then—depending on wind directions/speed/variability—blanket a huge area. Invisible, fallout will kill and sicken. It can be detected only by instruments carried by civil defense/police/military.

WARNINGS

Period of increasing tension in the daily news is first likely indication. Official instructions will be given by radio/TV/press/noticeboards if things get really bad.

Official U.S. Civil Defense warning system is siren sound for 5 to 7 minutes. Public takes shelter and receives further instructions through Emergency Radio Broadcasting System.

WHAT TO DO WHEN WARNED

BAD NEWS

Make home as fireproof (see *TOO BRIGHT/TOO HOT*) and *falloutproof* as possible. Working fast you can do a great deal towards this in a day. Stock with supplies.

If you live in cottage, single story prefabricated house or mobile home, try to join families in more substantial dwellings.

Middle floors of multistory apartments are the safest, while ground and top floors (especially top) are unsafe. Occupants here should join families on middle floors if possible.

Apartments four stories high or less, however, are safe only on the ground floor.

ADVANCE PREPARATIONS

Preparing against first flash-heat wave (see *TOO BRIGHT/TOO HOT*).

MAKING A FALLOUT REFUGE

Effects of fallout can be weakened by three factors.
1. DISTANCE
2. THICKNESS
3. TIME

Choose cellar/room/passage with fewest outside walls. Try to buttress walls/windows/doors with as much extra thickness as possible. Bricks, concrete, hard-packed earth all baffle fallout attack.

(a) Hole in ground outdoors (roofed with boards and soil), cellar or basement give best protection.

(b) Room on ground floor of house with as little outside wall as possible can be used. Or an interior passage. The further away from outside walls and roof you are the better.

(c) Thinly protected house can give some shelter if you build a fallout refuge core (see later).

Put as much distance between you and the outside of the house as possible. Strengthen and thicken all around the refuge. Take out windows and fill spaces with double layer of bricks, or board up and pack in between with hard-packed soil. Wire or bolt boards together.

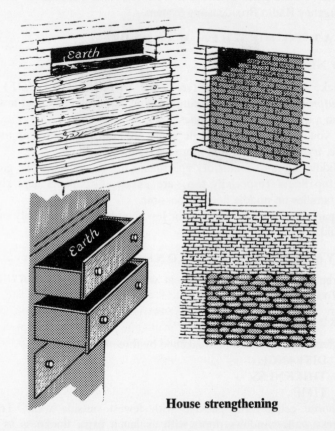

House strengthening

Pile up heavy furniture/books/sandbags against windows, doors and walls. Block windows and doors of rooms and/or passages leading to fallout refuge. Pile sandbags/earth boxes/oil drums on outside of refuge walls. Deep snow also helps.

An outdoor trench deep enough for family to stand in is very effective. Shore sides with improvised pit props. Cover top with planks/

metal sheeting/concrete slabs, then pile and press down soil on top.

Keep tools inside (in case you have to dig out). Manhole entrance through roof can be covered with garbage-can lid (covered on top with anything convenient).

If you make passage it may collapse under blast. Jam sandbags to prop its roof and combat radiation.

Outdoor fallout shelter

MAKING REFUGE CORE

Build another shelter inside refuge to give extra protection (especially during first three days of fallout). It can vary from tent of sandbags to a lean-to formed by doors propped against the wall and covered with sandbags, cushions filled with earth, plastic bags full of soil.

An underfloor trench covered over is effective. So is closet under stairs with sandbags covering all stairs and built up outside walls.

After three days, worst of fallout could be over, allowing you to live in rest of refuge before going outdoors at (approximately) the end of ten days.

STOCKING UP

Use a check list of equipment needed in refuge. You must be self-sufficient. Don't take so much stuff that the place becomes cluttered, but use common sense.

Remember you will be using this small place for sleeping/eating and as bathroom and lavatory. A radio is essential. So is plenty of fresh water and food (all kept in tightly sealed containers). Hygiene is very important too.

Fallout shelter cores

FOOD AND WATER

Supplies should last three weeks at least.

Food and water are *not* contaminated by radiation rays passing through. But will be contaminated once *fallout dust collects on it.*

Always wipe off food and water containers before opening. Water kept in open-topped containers (like the bath) must be covered, and the top wiped before it is lifted off.

Remember—it is essential to cut off water main as soon as the first warning is heard, so contaminated supply cannot enter and spoil water already in your cistern/lavatory/pipes.

Keep at least three-day supply of water (which is more important than food) in refuge core. Wipe off and take care when opening container that no fallout dust can spill inside.

A search for food outdoors (see *TOO EMPTY*) following fallout period means you must look for foods naturally protected—like nuts, say, which are shielded by the shell. WHEN POSSIBLE CHECK FOODS WITH AUTHORITIES. Wear gloves when handling.

(a) Eggs will probably be safe to eat—especially if hens stayed under cover during fallout.

(b) Wash and peel potatoes (fallout contamination is not removed by cooking alone). Cook.

(c) Peas and beans protected by their pods would be edible.

(d) Green like cabbages/Brussels sprouts/lettuces are fairly safe. Pick the heart and discard all outer leaves. Note: Hearts must be solid and have been shielded by outer leaves.

(e) Fish will probably be safe to eat.

(f) No animals which have been roaming outside through fallout period will be safe.

But after first few days of fallout there is risk of plants being contaminated by their roots taking up radioactive material in the soil.

If food so scarce you must eat growing plants (and there is no chance of having them tested) eat in this order: (1) potatoes, (2) peas, (3) beans, (4) greens.

Water in supply mains will be contaminated. And rain water too. Boiling water does not make it fit to drink. Water in wells/caves/tanks will probably be drinkable however. Water from lakes/rivers/canals can be filtered after a fashion by digging hole about a pace away from the bank. Muddy water will seep into hole. Let it stand until clear. Purify (see *TOO DRY*).

(Note: When going outside after fallout has faded, follow official instructions on safety precautions. Dress so outer clothing can still be left outside shelter on return—including shoes and boots. Always wear gloves indoors or out when handling anything that could have been contaminated by fallout.)

CAUGHT IN WILDERNESS COUNTRY

Take shelter—in caves/under rock overhangs/inside gorges/below downed trees. Go to ground and become falloutproof.

Out in open . . . lie down; brush ground clean; scrape shallow trench; build wall right around you as you lie; roof yourself with whatever handy—tent material/parachute/plastic sheet. Keep knocking fabric roof from underneath to decontaminate it by shaking off particles which settle on it.

Sod walls are O.K. in bog or hard-frozen settings. Different materials need certain thicknesses to be radiationproof. Examples: Snow must be 20-feet thick: ice, about height of a man; rock, length of a baseball bat; earth, a yard deep.

Make shelter warm and comfortable as possible. Stay INSIDE for at least two weeks. Only go outside when desperate for water.

RADIATION SICKNESS

Could be slight or serious. Signs: sickness, weakness, nausea, diarrhea, loss of appetite, possibly delirium.

Treat wounds or other injuries; remove all contaminated clothing where possible and wash patient—remembering the hair. Wear gloves/long coat/mask.

Keep patient's clothing and washing water separate from anything else to avoid contamination danger.

Await help from police/civil defense/military.

14: TOO EMPTY

Hunger alone does not kill. Man can stay alive several weeks without solid food, but he will grow so weak he becomes increasingly prey to sickness/disease/elements.

After his ordeal a survivor's condition will depend on what he found to eat. And how he overcame his distaste of accessible meals like cockroaches, frogs, nettles, birds.

To detail what is SAFE to eat would take books (there are over 300,000 plants alone). What basic rules can the survivor follow to stave off starvation when on the spot?

LIVE OFF THE LAND

Eat as much and whenever possible (unless short of water). Try for one hot meal a day minimum.

Keep in reserve whatever food you already have (follow directions on survival food packs). Spin it out with the food you find.

Grass. Ferns. Tree bark. Eggs. Shellfish. Slugs. Candles. Lizards. Frogs. Seaweed. Squirrels. Crickets. Rats. Termites. Grasshoppers. Seagulls. And thousands more.

Stick mainly to plant-eating when short on water. Plants won't increase thirst as much as fish/meat/eggs (see *TOO DRY*).

If it moves—consider it potentially rich food. Exceptions: all toads, some shellfish, some salt-water fish, and parts of various creatures like the liver of polar bears and seals, skin of salamanders, heads of snakes.

PLANTS

TEST

1. PLANT MUST NOT IRRITATE SKIN/SMELL/HAVE MILKY JUICE.
2. BITE OFF SMALL PIECE.

3. HOLD PIECE INSIDE LOWER LIP FOR FIVE MINUTES.
4. EAT THIS IF NO SOAPY/BITTER/BURNING TASTE.
5. IF NO ILL EFFECTS WITHIN TEN HOURS PLANT IS SAFE.

Some plants which are safe to eat won't pass this test (see later), but majority of plants do.

Small quantity of poisonous food is unlikely to kill or make you seriously ill whereas large dose will. Once plant passes test don't eat large quantities at once, but gradually increase quantities.

Plants eaten by birds and animals are not always safe for humans. Test these plants as you would any other before eating in quantity.

Avoid mushrooms—unless you *know* them to be safe.

All plants should be cooked for safety—especially when you are not sure. But poisonous mushrooms are not made safe by cooking.

Experiment with best parts of plants to eat: fruit; bark, sap; tubers; roots; seeds; pods; flowers; buds; nuts; leaves; stems; bulbs; shoots.

WIDESPREAD PLANTS

Universally-found edible plants (see later for plants special to areas) are:

(a) Grasses (including rice/oats/wheat). Pile grass onto cloth and beat out seeds with stick. Rub/shred/blow chaff away and pound seeds in container. Boil or roast (avoid black and withered seeds). Stems are edible too.

(b) Nuts everywhere can be eaten. Bitter taste can be washed away by swilling mashed-up nuts in a stream.

(c) Tree bark (inner layers) is edible boiled/roasted/chewed raw. Avoid only if unpleasantly bitter.

(d) Berries should be tested carefully first—they may be poisonous even though birds eat them.

(e) Ferns (especially the young coils) are a safe stand-by. Scrub away hairs in water and boil.

(f) Elephant grass (in all damp areas) grows taller than a man and has seeds like firework sparklers. Boil roots/flowers/shoots.

(g) Bamboo has many edible parts: seeds/shoots/roots. This grass grows from tall swamp grasses to trees over 100 feet high. And grows wherever really moist and warm.

(h) Seaweed clinging to rocks or floating is edible when healthy/fresh/firm (though will make you thirsty). Leave slimy, decaying seaweed alone.

(i) Lichens can be scraped/peeled/crumbled off rock and soaked well in water. Boil.

HUNTING

Small animals and insects are your most likely bet. View hunting with common sense. Don't expect success at first. But something to come slowly with practice.

WEAPONS

Use everything. Catapaults powered by underpants elastic or hide from already dead animals. Clubs/bludgeons/spears. Knives. Rock missiles. Sling/bow and arrow/gun.

Keep knives sharp. Any sandstone will do this, but gray soft sandstone better than quartz (which will scratch knife blade with bright scars).

Granite (rubbed smooth on another granite lump) will also sharpen knives. Hold blade at slight angle on stone and push away, sharpening sides alternately.

Keep guns clean. Never clog the barrel—or try to shoot out an obstruction. Clean barrel with hot water and pull through piece of cloth on string.

In arctic cold clean all oil off gun. Wrap it well against any contact with snow or ice. Leave wrapped outside a warm shelter.

GOING FOR THE KILL

Least subtle approach best when inexperienced. Arm companions with clubs and/or net. Surround area of bush. Set fire to target and attack creatures which run out. If no fire, converge, trampling down undergrowth.

Other variations: Set fire to hollow tree; poke sticks down holes having sealed off as many other exits from a warren as you can find; or light fire at burrow entrance. Wait with weapons for animal to come out.

Fire catapault/sling/gun as close to target as possible. Aim to make one shot do the job. And fire from steadiest position you can find.

Shoulder/chest/head are best all-round targets of game. If animal/bird/reptile falls reload immediately and be ready for it to get up and run.

Try to catch your target lying/sitting/standing. This needs very careful approach:

(a) Discover where animals pass. Signs are droppings, tracks, trampled ground. Best areas: water/forest clearings/edges of thickets.

(b) Avoid the trail or runway itself once discovered. Prepare to hunt in early morning or dusk.

(c) Hide with face to wind or the slightest breeze. If sun shining keep it behind you if possible.

(d) Keep still.

(e) *Crawl* forward only when animal is feeding/drinking/looking away. As soon as it starts to turn head freeze.

(f) Avoid snapping twigs, brushing aside foliage, silhouetting yourself.

Try night hunting with a light. It can attract creatures, giving you chance to strike/club/spear. You will develop various methods with practice—like stalking a frog with one hand while grabbing with the other.

TRAPPING

Success is bound to be hit and miss until you are well practiced. But you may be lucky. Make a determined search for signs of wildlife in your region.

Use lots of snares/traps/deadfalls to capture, strangle or crush wild creatures. Diagrams show principles of how these work and can be improvised, but use common sense. For instance saplings bent over and tied to a snare may not budge if triggered by animal in very cold weather (trees are frozen stiff).

Keep traps simple and small. You are unlikely to trap big animals with cumbersome and elaborate deadfalls.

Elastic/cord/wire are essentials. So are *natural*-looking traps. Lay them across narrowest part of trails and runways. Or narrow down a wide trail with rocks/foliage/herbages—so long as it looks part of area.

Lie in cover, keep still, watch for signs of life when you have found tracks. One kind of animal life usually means other forms around too. Snares can be hand-held ready to pull.

(Note: Snares across tracks or over animal burrows should admit creature's head but be too small for the body.)

Wild life can be attracted towards a trap by kissing back of hand to make loud squeaks.

Butcher a trapped animal on the spot and leave entrails. These may attract other animals within several hours. Reset trap.

Traps and triggers

FISHING

Most fish are edible—poisonous ones are found mainly in tropical waters close to land. Remember when short of water—eating fish will increase thirst.

WHERE TO LOOK

Deepest parts of rivers. Pools below rapids in shallow streams. Behind and under rocks. Below the bank. Underneath falls. Experiment at all likely places.

Fish with outgoing tide. Remember one of best regions for food is between high and low water mark.

Fish in early morning or dusk. Fish are attracted by a light. Flying fish can be landed on a raft by reflecting flashlight or moonlight onto sail/shirt/sheet and catching them as they jump.

Shrimps, prawns, crabs, crayfish can be caught by combination of shining a light, searching shallow waters and using nets.

Watch swimming habits of fish, type of food they are likely to go for, then use your ingenuity to net/hook/trap them.

CATCHING FISH

Line and hook can be improvised with cloth or plant fibers and bent pin (though proper hooks much better). Try different lures: feathers/plastic/fish entrails or bright cloth, metal or worms.

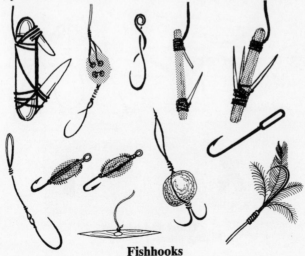

Fishhooks

Hooks can be made from bone/wire/wood. Stop fishing line being bitten through by attaching hook to line with thin wire.

Jerk heavy metal bait up and down in water to attract fish. (Hooks and lure must be heavy enough to sink quickly.)

A small kite (see *TOO LONELY*) will carry a fishing line well out over water and increases your chances. Rig fishing line to kite line with bent pin at one place only—and so any tension (from biting fish) to fishing line will jerk it free. Or you release it yourself.

Other methods:

(a) Catch by tickling fish under rocks with bare hands. Then scoop out.

(b) Wade into shallow water and club/spear/net fish. Or do it from the bank.

(c) Stun fish in pools and ponds by burning coral or seashells to make lime and throwing into water.

(d) Make nets from whatever line/string/cordage handy. Parachute cloth net for shrimping. Close-mesh net can be stretched out across stream between two of you walking quickly through it lifting rocks in water, snatching net out frequently with a possible catch each time.

A gill net hangs in still lake/river/sea water and traps fish swimming through it. Fix under ice as shown with branches/sticks/poles and patience. Set net at right angles to shore. Use stones for weights and wood/rubber/cork for float.

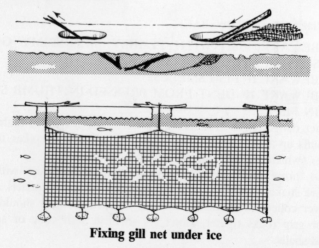

Fixing gill net under ice

(e) Fish traps can be made from rocks and sticks (as shown). Check movements of schools of fish. Sea fish often move in with the tide and swim along the shore. Lake fish come towards banks in morning and at dusk.

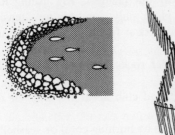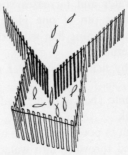

Fish traps

Pick trap site at high tide and build at low. Make it look as much a part of the scenery as possible. Use any natural features—spits/reefs/ledges—as part of trap. Look at it from fish's viewpoint.

Nets work all the time, and traps store fish fresh and live until you need them. They could prove worth the trouble they are to make.

CATCHES TO THROW BACK

1. BEWARE FISH WITH FLABBY SKIN/SLIMY GILLS/ SUNKEN EYES.
2. BEWARE IF FISH SMELLS.
3. BEWARE IF DENT FROM PRESSED-IN THUMB STAYS IN FISH.

Other danger signs are: naked or bony skin instead of scales; fish that puffs up as it is taken from water; fish covered in spikes/thorns/ bristles (which can give you poisonous wound).

Also throw back netted jellyfish/diamond-shaped rays with long tails/sea snakes (they have flat tails). Keep off black mussels.

Never collect dead shellfish—when touched shellfish should move and/or grip rocks tighter. Don't try shellfish with cone or spindle-shaped shells.

COOKING

1. CLEAN FOOD SOON AFTER COLLECTING.
2. ALWAYS COOK WHEN POSSIBLE.
3. DRY EXTRA MEAT OR FISH OVER FIRE OR IN SUN.

Remove poisonous parts of creature at once (say head of snake). Slit animal's stomach and roll skin backwards like taking off glove. Scrape skin and guts.

Shell food (clams/oysters/mussels/crabs/crayfish) should be left overnight in clean water (salt or fresh) to clean themselves.

Crabs/crayfish/lobsters should be cooked alive—or shortly after death. They spoil rapidly.

Scale and wash fish in clean water. Cut out gills and slit underside. Chop head off.

Boiling is best way of cooking in survival situations. If possible drink the cooking water too. Boil sea food in sea water. Add plants to fish or meat stews.

If no cooking pot available use improvised spit or fork to roast over coals. Or wrap in clay/mud/wet leaves and bake among hot embers— don't clean or skin food before baking. Or make utensils from inner layers of birch bark (as shown).

If no fire available in very cold conditions let food freeze, then carve off thin shavings, warming it to just below freezing before eating.

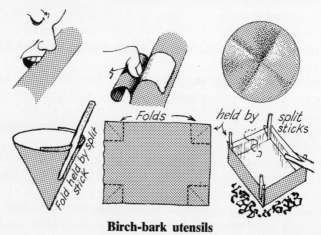

Birch-bark utensils

STORING FOOD

Keep fish alive in trap until you need it. Or store in box underwater. Once dead—like meat—cut into strips and dry under hot sun or fire smoke if unable to boil it right away.

Cover food. Wrap it against insect and animal contamination. Hang on trees out of animal reach.

Use damp packing: shellfish in seaweed; berries/fruit/roots in sphagnum moss, wet leaves. Keep food cool in holes in ground/banks/rocks. Wet-cloth hole cover acts as cooler. Food stays fresh buried in snow or sand (but mark the spot).

Wipe off mold on stored meat. In wet conditions smoked or sundried meat and fish need drying out to prevent mold. In hot weather recook once-cooked animal food once a day.

Best safeguard of all against food poisoning is to eat *fresh* food.

ASPECTS OF FOOD FINDING

ARCTIC

You need more food in cold climate than in hot. Yet here food can be very scarce (although plentiful in sub-arctic areas).

Marmots, squirrels, rabbits, hares, porcupines, muskrats, rats, beavers, geese—all possible prey. Obviously avoid the big food (polar bears) unless you have gun, skill and courage.

Fishing through ice is determined by whether you can find a place thin enough to chop through. Use line or net (see earlier).

Vegetation is sometimes abundant, sometimes hidden. Watch where birds land.

Eat lichens/seaweed/roots/greens/berries. But leave fungi alone.

DESERT

Food should only be eaten in small doses when water is short (see *TOO DRY*).

Plant food is rare. Try cacti fruit/roots/leaves (with spikes removed). Greenest grass is food source too. Avoid plants with milky sap.

Gazelle/antelope/birds sometimes seen near water. But most likely animal foods are snakes/rats/lizards/slugs/locusts—if you are lucky.

DESERT ISLANDS

Seafood is most reliable—so long as nonpoisonous. Clams, mussels, sea cucumbers, crabs, sea urchins, crayfish, shrimps can be found on shore and in coral-reef pockets.

Avoid black mussels and shellfish with cone-shaped or spindly shells.

Follow turtle tracks on sand. Turtles can be rolled on their backs (watch claws and mouth). Cut off heads and bake. Eggs may be buried near sea and 2 feet under sand.

Even barren islands often have edible weeds—some with yellow flowers tasting like watercress. Coconut palms and screw-pine palms (with good fruit looking like pineapples) found on otherwise bare islands too.

JUNGLE

Many foods are available in jungle, though hard to find in rain forest. Old native gardens (abandoned) are excellent food source. Test all plants you try (as earlier).

(a) Coconuts are a standby for food (see *TOO DRY*).

(b) Sago palm has spiny trunk. Grind up pith under bark, soak in water, strain and bake residue.

(c) Taro roots/leaves/stalks must be boiled. Leaves are shaped like elephant ears.

(d) Papaya is oblong-shaped fruit on palm-type tree (avoid leaves which have milky sap).

(e) Mangoes also exception to milky-sap rule. They grow on knobbly-trees with dense canopy, and resemble large pears.

(f) Figs (edible grow on milky-sap trees).

(g) Breadfruit (milky sap) looks like yellowy-green melon on leathery-leaved tree.

(h) Yams (like potatoes) have to be dug from under plants with gigantic and coarse leaves.

Bananas/sugar cane/pineapple add to the wide variety of edible tropical plants ranging from bamboo and grass to water lilies and ferns.

Avoid:

Milky-sap plants apart from exceptions mentioned
Fungi

Plants which irritate/burn/wound your skin
Anything tasting foul
Plants resembling tomatoes
Brightly colored fruits and berries

Monkeys' food is a fairly reliable pointer to safe human food, but still test first.

Small creatures (frogs, lizards, snakes, insects, grubs, birds) much more likely to provide meals than big game.

MOUNTAINS

Very little food on high ridges besides lichens and birds. Descend below tree line to eat.

HUNGER HAZARDS

POISONING

Need not be in the wilds. If not, telephone doctor immediately. Do what he says.

Otherwise drink *lots* of water (or milk) to dilute. Make yourself vomit by sticking fingers down throat. Salt and water (warmed) do same job.

After vomiting, drink more milk. Four glasses say.

Note: If poisoned by acid, alkali (ammonia), gasoline or kerosene, don't try to be sick. Acid—two teaspoonfuls of magnesia in glass of water; alkalis—teaspoonful of vinegar in glass of water; gasoline or kerosene—lots of glasses of water.

WAYS TO TELL IF CANNED FOOD IS SAFE

If it smells all right—food is O.K. Note: Food (apart from canned fruit) can be kept short time in an *opened* can.

BUT if a can bulges outwards at either or both ends it is "blown"—definitely not fit to eat.

CANNIBALISM

(See *TOO CROWDED*.)

AFTERWORD

A LAST CHANCE

Can you be sure someone IS dead?

Not always. It can puzzle even medical people sometimes. Example: People suffering extreme exposure (see *TOO COLD*) resemble corpses. Look at the hours and hours it has sometimes taken to bring around an apparently had-it person with artificial respiration.

In certain cases signs of death can be misleading if taken individually. Blue lips might simply mean blockage in airways. Waxy skin (or pallor) could be caused by bleeding. You may be missing the beating of the heart if you are not feeling in the right place. (To do this: Place pads of fingertips on skin of lower left chest and feel over a wide region.)

Play safe. Look for as many signs of death as possible, thus:

No heartbeat
No pulse
Blue lips
Pallor
Muscles stiff
Bowel movement
Mouth agape
Dilated pupils
Pupils don't move in flashlight
Eyes glazed
Body cold
Muscle stays flat after pressed
Skin stained reddish blue in parts
No blurring on mirror held to nose/mouth

Unless there is no doubt at all that a person is dead, keep up artificial respiration/keeping them warm/getting help quickly. Or whatever else circumstances dictate. And REALLY KEEP IT UP—right to the bitter end.

THE FINAL WORD

Lest the reader be left cowering and broken—and quite unfit to survive—after a book of such unrelieved disaster, fire, flood and mayhem, let me close with the words that introduced the book:

ALL THE *ABOVE* ADVICE
PRESUPPOSES THAT
WHOEVER FACES CATASTROPHE
TAKES A DEEP BREATH
AND MAKES UP HIS MIND
TO HAVE A REALLY DETERMINED GO
AT BEATING THE ODDS

Survival belongs not to the strong but to the prepared.
Good health.

INDEX